ABELARD
AND
HELOISE

DONALD E. ERICSON

ABELARD
and
HELOISE

Their Lives, Their Love,
Their Letters

BENNETT-EDWARDS
Publishers
NEW YORK, N. Y.

Library of Congress Catalog Card Number 89-82393

ISBN 0-9617271-1-X

Also by Donald E. Ericson
THE PORTUGUESE LETTERS

PRINTED IN THE UNITED STATES OF AMERICA

THESE PAGES, long in the making, are dedicated to my mother and to my wife. Early on, my mother instilled her love of learning in her children—for this I owe her a debt of gratitude. I am, however, particularly grateful to my wife for having given me her unwavering support—her efforts have been so many and so varied that it is not possible to enumerate them.

P R E F A C E

THE TRAGEDY of Pierre Abelard, a young Breton scholar, and his loving Heloise is centuries old. While the outer forms of our culture may have altered, the spirit which moved that famous pair is still alive. The poignant story of their trials and tribulations is contained in a series of letters they wrote, in Latin, over eight hundred years ago. The first one, addressed to a friend, contained Abelard's autobiography and is known as the 'Historia Calamitatum' (Story of My Misfortunes). It does not appear here in letter form, but is incorporated in "The Story of Their Lives." The other letters were exchanges between Heloise and her scholar-husband. Strangely enough, the correspondence began only after their ill-fated marriage and enforced separation, long after Heloise had entered a cloister and Abelard had become a monk.

The epistles were first translated into French by Jean de Meung at the end of the thirteenth century. In 1616 the publication of d'Amboise and Duchesne appeared in Paris. There followed, among others, the Watts edition in London in 1722, which received extraordinary acclaim, although the letters had been paraphrased rather than translated. Not only was the spirit of the original superbly preserved, but the manner in which events were presented was thought highly effective. It is in part this edition which is used as the basis for the rendition that follows.

F O R E W O R D

WHEN I BEGAN to put on paper the story of Abelard and Heloise, it was not my intention to explore every aspect of their lives. In fact, I avoided the pronouncements on philosophy and the questions of theology so profusely addressed by others, unless they played an inherent part in the tragic events which had shaped the destiny of the celebrated pair.

My purpose in these pages, then, is to record the joys and sorrows of the lovers and to render a simple account of their experiences. Thus I have tried to recount their history in as unencumbered a fashion as I would have liked to read it, ever since I first became aware of their existence.

It was in Paris, in the Library of Stê. Genevieve, that I accidentally came across their correspondence. Apparently the small book had been misplaced, possibly due to a similarity in subject matter to that of a volume I had been trying to locate. The book for which I had been searching was the personal account of the life of Mariana Alcoforado, a 17th-century Portuguese nun who, like Heloise, had been a far-famed victim of masculine selfishness.

As I leafed, captivated, through the pages, reading the letters Heloise had written to her erstwhile lover, I was unaware that the library in which I found myself stood on Mont Stê. Genevieve (as this modest rise was known in medieval times.) Quite possibly I was on the very site where the handsome Breton scholar, who called himself Abelard, had lectured to huge audiences of enthusiastic students.

His fame as an outstanding and provocative teacher immeasurably contributed to the city's reputation as a center of learning, a distinction Paris holds, in many respects, to this day. It was also he who had paved the way for the re-appearance of the philosophy of Aristotle, whose rational concepts became so firmly entrenched at the end of the twelfth century. Further, I should not fail to mention that it was Abelard, more than anyone, who had given impetus to the academic movement leading to the later founding of the University of Paris, the institution which was to serve as the model and prototype for most universities in Europe. The venerable school, though its appearance has changed, still stands around the corner from the library and is better known as the Sorbonne.

To be sure, Abelard's achievements were of notable importance to his time and to the centuries which followed; but it is Heloise, her selfless devotion and her infinite compassion for the man she loved, who transcends the ages.

AVENTURA, January 1990

PIERRE ABELARD was born in the last quarter of the eleventh century in the small town of Le Pallet, about nine miles from Nantes in Brittany. He was the oldest son of Berenger, a nobleman and a knight in the service of Hoel, Duke of Brittany. Besides Abelard, there were three other sons: Radulphus, Dagobert and Porcarius; then there was a daughter by the name of Denise. Abelard's mother, of whom he spoke with great tenderness, was Lucia.

Berenger had been a man of some culture. Abelard said of him that, before "girding himself with the soldier's belt,"[1] his father had been interested in the study of theology. It follows then that he wanted his sons, especially the eldest and most promising, to receive an education before joining the soldiers' ranks.

Abelard's scholastic enthusiasm, however, ran counter to his father's plans: not only was he discontent with the modicum of knowledge Berenger had intended for him, but soldiering was not to his taste. He preferred, he wrote, "to fight his battles with the weapons of reason rather than with weapons of war."[2]

Regrettably, Abelard tells us nothing of his childhood and since most of his history comes from his own narrative, our knowledge of his early youth is scant, very scant indeed.

This account begins about the year 1095, when for most men knowledge and scholarship were still very limited and life was harsh and full of hazards. But for some time European scholars had been probing the lands which lay beyond the continent's eastern boundaries. Arab translations of the scientific and philosophical works of the Greek thinkers had long been in evidence in the enlightened Islamic world. The scholarship of Baghdad and Damascus, of Toledo and Seville in Islamic Spain, was beginning to reach the learning centers of Christian Europe. Though fragments of the treatises of Aristotle had been known in the West in earlier centuries, the latest uncoverings of Hellenic wisdom shed fresh light on thoughts and events of the past and played a significant role in influencing the evolving scholastic renaissance. With it, a new spirit pervaded society. The educated youth of Europe, still few in number, was gripped with a boundless thirst for knowledge: a ray of reason was about to penetrate medieval darkness.

Seized by the learning fever of his day, Abelard decided, at the age of sixteen, to leave the comfort of his father's castle and strike out on his own. He told us he had chosen to forgo his inheritance and the privileges of the first-born in favor of the quest for "truth and knowledge."[3] Clad in the coarse tunic of the pilgrim, prudently void of pockets in the custom of the time, he journeyed freely and unmolested over the unpaved roads of the land. Now and then, a lord or a wealthy merchant in his finery, his heavily laden vehicle protected by dauntless bodyguards, would hurry by; or one might meet a hapless clerk jogging along on his burro, anxiously watching the woods alongside the road ahead. With scarcely more than a bundle of food slung over his shoulder, a student, on the other hand, had little to fear from roaming bands of robbers who, often in the service of a local seigneur, plundered the passing traveler —an affliction which would plague the countryside throughout medieval times.

We now come upon Abelard at Loches, in the lecture halls of Jean Roscelin. The reputed Rationalist was a rebel with a cause, a scholar who had employed Aristotelian logic in opposition to long-established dogma. This was the discipline which, early in his career, had led Roscelin to question the sacred doctrine of the Trinity. For that offense the Church had banned him from France, forcing him to settle beyond the reach of the royal writ for a number of years.

There is some disagreement as to the length of time Roscelin had been Abelard's instructor, but there is no doubt that the younger Breton followed in his master's wake and that his own rational endeavors, leading to his subsequent confrontations with church authorities, were directly rooted in Roscelin's teachings. Later on, however, an exchange of letters suggests that Abelard, by now Master Abelard, and his former teacher had an ideological falling-out of no small proportion.

During the next few years Abelard became a 'wandering scholar,' a part of that throng of boys and men who travelled unceasingly through the far-flung provinces of France. Go-

ing from one episcopal town to another, he
made his way from school to school, attracted
to wherever "dialectics flourished or a notable
teacher held forth."[4] With the exception of
mathematics, for which he seems to have had
no inclination, Abelard was proud of his intellectual powers. He appears to have taken keen
delight in testing his rhetorical skills by engag-
ing his masters in open discussions and turning
ordinary debates into scholarly duels.

At the age of twenty Abelard arrived in Paris.
There was no sign as yet of the ecclesiastical
architecture to come, or the enormity of buildings to be constructed along the valley of the
Seine. For now, almost all of Paris still lay
on the largest of the three islands, known to
us as the Ile de la Cité. It should be mentioned
that there was an extraordinary number of
abbeys to be found here. Each abbey had its
own school attached and, because of the outstanding quality of some of the masters who
taught there, the city was, even in those early
times, beginning to turn into a hub of scholastic philosophy.

In medieval Paris the life of a student was
an arduous one: "at five or six o'clock each

morning the great Cathedral bell would ring
out the summons to work. From the neighboring houses of the canons, from the cottages of
the townsfolk, from the taverns and hospices
and boarding-houses, the stream of the industrious would pour into the enclosure beside the
Cathedral."[5] The routine would seldom vary:
in the lecture hall, before collecting the tuition
for the day, the master's assistant would strew
either hay or straw on the floor, depending on
the time of year. The teacher would sit in the
only chair available, and after his assistant had
brought him his book with his notes, the latter
would direct his energies toward quelling the
street noises from outside. The students surrounding the massive chair would be, literally,
at their master's feet. "Sitting on their haunches,
the right knee raised to serve as a desk for the
waxed tablets, they would take notes during
the long hours of lectures (about six or seven),
then hurry home—if they were industrious—to
commit them to parchment while the light
lasted."[6]

Our young scholar had eagerly turned in the
direction of a particular institution, the celebrated cloister-school of Notre Dame, where

18

William of Champeaux was both master and unchallenged academic benefactor. While Abelard acknowledged William's reputation as the day's leading dialectician (as expounders of logic were called), the master's unyielding defense of Plato's lofty precepts fell far short of the budding scholar's more earthly Aristotelian orientation. At first merely questioning William's philosophy, he soon ventured to challenge the master and relentlessly embarrassed him by pointing to gross inconsistencies in his arguments. Not unexpectedly, Abelard's activism eventually caused considerable friction among his fellow-students; in particular, some of the older ones who backed their teacher, resented the audacity and the conceit of the younger newcomer. The enthusiastic encouragement many of his other comrades displayed whenever Abelard out-reasoned William served only to heighten the tension. As feuding among the students grew increasingly unruly, the young noble, who had at first been warmly received, had become a source of great vexation to the master. It was here, at this juncture, Abelard later wrote, the calamities of his life had their beginnings.

19

To break free from the turbulent environment he would unfailingly create for himself, Abelard turned his back on the city and, with the support of several fellow-students, opened his own academy. The site he chose for this rival venture was Melun, one of the principal royal seats, about thirty miles from Paris.

All agree Abelard was a brilliant and charismatic instructor, quick of mind and without peer in the art of disputation. To this we must add a melodious voice and the facility to deliver his lectures with sublime clarity. As for William, he was a conservative dialectician, resolutely committed to orthodox elucidation. His lessons were stilted and confined to a narrow path of long-established rhetoric: dogma could not be tampered with and authoritative statements were considered valid proof of 'truth.' Abelard, on the other hand, free of undue piety, encouraged his audiences to doubt—to avoid false conclusions by debating the pros and cons of an issue, even when the subject matter was of sacred origin. The effect of the new logic was electrifying and brought about a profound change in attitude among the student population of Paris. They wanted rational explanations rather than words which defied reason, and held with Abelard that it was absurd for anyone to teach to others what he himself did not comprehend.

From the flow of competing students zealously exchanging opinions as they went back and forth between Notre Dame and Abelard's academy at Melun, it soon became apparent that a great many deserted their old master in favor of Abelard's open forums. Infuriated by the exodus of his pupils and the no less important loss of fees, William importuned the royal courts to suppress Abelard's classes. But his attempts failed: apparently William had argued with and offended some of the King's courtiers, who responded by denying his request and backing the younger scholar.

Still, Abelard was not satisfied. Emboldened by his success and sure of his abilities, he now sought closer proximity to Paris. He was confident that the time saved by a shorter journey to his lectures would permit more frequent debates with the students and would give him the opportunity to bring a greater number of them into his fold. It would also bring him closer to his objective of driving his opponent from his

21

stronghold at Notre Dame. Consequently he transferred his classroom halfway back to the city, to Corbeil, another busy royal freehold.

It was not by accident that the young teacher established himself within the environs of royal estates. He had friends at Court, people on whose support he could rely. Times were perilous and punishment severe when thinking varied from the prescribed dogma of the Church; royal patronage, with the protection the royal Court afforded, was therefore an essential safeguard, especially for one who freely spoke his mind and embroiled himself in theological frays as often as Abelard did.

With the Breton scholar once more moving closer, William became alarmed. Fearing his life's work threatened, he availed himself of every underhanded method to sabotage Abelard's teaching efforts. Rivalry turned into fierce animosity and as clashes between their respective followers became more violent, Abelard withdrew and dropped from sight. Perhaps fearful of the intrigues of his opponents, he recorded only that he had fallen ill and returned to Brittany, but gave no details of the five or six years he spent there, nor did he mention the nature of his 'ailment.' We may safely assume, however, that, driven as he was, he had not been idle, for when he reappeared in Paris, he was well prepared to debate his concepts and seek victory over his rivals.

During Abelard's absence the Bishop of Paris had elevated William to the office of Archdeacon. Setting his sights on still higher office and affecting an air of greater piety, William then placed an alternate in his chair at the school of Notre Dame and entered the haven of a small priory of the monks of St. Victor. His altered circumstances, however, did not lessen William's worldly interests and he continued his public lectures in the very priory which he had ostensibly entered for the sole purpose of a life of prayer and contemplation.

Undaunted by William's new station, Abelard soon created an opportunity to debate his former teacher once again. Mingling with a group of friars and clerics, he joined William's courses in the priory at St. Victor and, after a few weeks of pretense at study, openly challenged the master to modify his definition of what in philosophical terms had been called 'universals' (a topic of all-consuming interest in Abelard's

23

time, but with little meaning for us today). William now found himself in an indefensible position and was publicly compelled to acknowledge Abelard's concepts. His subsequent reversal in his interpretation of that passionately debated issue proved to be so humiliating a defeat that William was forced to renounce his leadership and give up his role as teacher. In turn, William's alternate at Notre Dame, seeing his master's authority in shambles and fearing an encounter with such a formidable antagonist as Abelard, avoided a confrontation by voluntarily abdicating the chair in his favor. A few days later, and as a further embarrassment to William, the alternate declared his support for Abelard by joining his classes. The Breton had scored an unequivocal victory.

But William's powerful influence was still in evidence and created new opposition. Not long after Abelard began his discourses at Notre Dame, the ecclesiastical establishment revoked his permission to teach and expelled him from the school. At this point, however, Abelard was not to be deterred. He returned to Melun, where he taught for a time. After an unsuccessful attempt to reclaim his chair at Notre Dame he

24

moved with his "army of students"[7] to the opposite bank of the river, to what was then the outskirts of Paris, to "set up camp"[8] on the summit of Mont Stê. Genevieve, referred to as 'the Hill' by Parisians.

At the foot of that historic hill, along the northern slope by the Seine, a new part of town was coming alive. Besides a bustling commercial center with crowded markets, hawking vendors, entertainers and innumerable craftsmen plying their trades, there were picturesque huddles of small buildings, chapels and brothels, hospices and schools. The students roaming through the streets were the sons of nobles and peasants, a vibrant and boisterous lot, garbed in multicolored tunics, gowns and hose. Though they had come from many lands of Europe, the language in which they all conversed and debated the urgent issues of the day was Latin. The gaily painted signs swinging above the tavern doors were inscribed in Latin and the songs coming from the bistros and sheltered gardens were in part French, but mostly Latin. This pattern was to persist, giving rise to the celebrated 'Latin Quarter,' truly Latin at that time.

Abelard's depiction of this period of his life remains vague, but we know it was from the top of the Hill, from the Abbey of Stê. Genevieve close to the present-day Pantheon, that he pursued his "assault"[9] on the champions of the old guard.

In the midst of that struggle for primacy of reason Abelard received an urgent request from his mother, asking him to come home to Brittany. His father, seeking his ultimate reward, had entered a monastery and Lucia, who had promised to do likewise, was about to retire to a convent. During that period it was not uncommon for elderly couples to retire to monastic societies in the eve of their lives. Evangelists of the day had broken up thousands of homes with their impassioned promises of an early reuniting in heaven, on the condition that husbands and wives first separate and enter religious institutions. "Home after home was left to the children and they, who had sworn companionship in life and death, cheerfully participated in this appalling dissolution of domestic ties and parted in the pathetic trust of a reunion."[10]

Abelard mentions the event but briefly. (We

can merely speculate how much it meant to him or to what extent it influenced his own decision later to enter a religious community.) After his mother was settled, rather than returning to his students at Mont Stê. Genevieve, Abelard abandoned them and moved on to Laon to study the Holy Scriptures.

His new teacher was the famous theologian Anselm. Despite the master's renown, Abelard seemed not to have been well-disposed toward him from the very start: "I stood before an old man who owed his name to his long-established presence rather than to his intellect. He was an extraordinary orator and his eloquence at first elicited admiration, but upon closer scrutiny his words were void of reason."[11] Just as Abelard had earlier confronted William by disputing his philosophical espousals, so now he challenged the rationality of Anselm's arguments. He showed little tolerance toward the old master and even less toward the students who supported him. Much to Abelard's grief, the hostilities he stirred up so blithely at Laon were to haunt him through many a long year.

It was a controversial and turbulent term for Abelard, but at its conclusion he had won an

27

academic triumph over Anselm and his followers. On his return to Paris, he found the climate changed. Opposition to his chair at Notre Dame had waned and the gates of the school were now open to him.

Abelard had overcome every obstacle and won every battle. He was the director of the schools of Paris and a canon of Notre Dame. For some time now he had been instructing in philosophy and theology to equal acclaim. No teacher since antiquity had held such sway and no other chair drew such crowds. While students in Paris had numbered in the hundreds at the beginning of the scholastic resurgence, during Abelard's academic rule they were counted by the thousands. With such a multitude of followers and the wealth they poured into his coffers, Abelard was, in fact, the undisputed master among the pedagogues of Paris; his fame had reached its peak. Referring to this period he later wrote, "Success swells the heads of fools. I flattered myself to be the only worthy philosopher in the world and saw no further threat to my position."[12]

We are told, though the testimony may well have been biased because it comes from the

28

pen of a loving woman, that besides Abelard's intellectual gifts, he was graced with charm and winning looks and whenever he appeared in public, women would yearn for him and follow him with longing eyes. Rumor has it that many had succumbed to his charms, but such tales are hard to prove. If we are to believe Abelard's own version, we must accept that he had never concerned himself with the opposite sex. He "abhorred the uncleanliness of prostitutes,"[13] he wrote and insisted that his conduct had been impeccable; that he had led a "purely academic and spiritual life."[14]

Around 1116 a radiant young girl named Heloise returned to Paris from a cloister school at Argenteuil, some few miles distant from the city. She lived on a corner of the rue de Chantres in the house of Fulbert, on one of the verdant islands of the Seine. Fulbert, a cleric and a canon of Notre Dame, is believed to have been her maternal uncle and guardian. Although almost nothing is known of Heloise's origin save that her mother's name was recorded in the chapel records of The Paraclete as Hersinde, one should not dismiss what had been suggested: that she was an illegitimate child. Most historians assume that she was born in or near Paris, about 1101, and that she was orphaned at an early age.

Some say that Fulbert was actually her father, although members of the clergy were not permitted to marry. The marriage ban was strictly enforced, particularly for those who sought advancement in the clerical hierarchy. Establishing an illicit relationship, however, and raising a family of "nieces and nephews" was condoned by the Church Fathers and did not necessarily constitute a threat to the attainment of higher office. Because Fulbert's position was an elevated one, it is reasonable to assume that if Heloise had indeed been his daughter, she would have been known as his niece. But other than the great affection he held for her, there is not the slightest evidence to support such speculation.

When Heloise first came into Abelard's life she was a charming and graceful sixteen-year-old, fluent in Latin and endowed with unequalled literary knowledge. Later chroniclers claimed she was also versed in Hebrew and Greek, and most likely she was, but the extent of her fluency in these languages has not been

ascertained. For a woman in the twelfth century to have an academic education was ex-
tremely rare, although some schools for women
existed in France, but to be so widely reputed
for her intellectual accomplishments at so young
an age was remarkable; it did not escape Master
Abelard's attention. He was intrigued and the
thought of bringing the young savante to his
bed played upon his pride. Abelard was now
about thirty-six years old. "I was handsome
enough" he wrote, "full of youth and had no
fear of being refused by any woman I might
choose to honor with my favors."[15]

Since Fulbert and Abelard were both canons
at the Cathedral, it was simple enough for the
scholar to obtain an invitation to Fulbert's home
to greet the acclaimed young newcomer from
Argenteuil. More than likely the older canon
felt gratified and greatly honored to have the
celebrated master as a guest at his table.

Details of Abelard's first encounter with
Heloise are not recorded, but afterward he
wrote that her literary accomplishment was not
the only attribute which appealed to him. It is
safe to assume he was delighted with the young
girl and was determined to see her again. The

31

scholar would have us believe that becoming Heloise's tutor was a stroke of good fortune, whereas it actually was a carefully thought-out plan to be near her and have access to her quarters. Recognizing the uncle's fondness for his gifted niece, and aware of his eagerness to further her education, Abelard placed his teaching skills at her disposal. It was a flattering offer—a temptation hard for a foolish old man to resist. The uncle's avarice seemed to have accomplished the rest, for Abelard would accept no fee for his instruction and, inasmuch as Fulbert's residence was so conveniently close to Abelard's school, he would pay handsomely for his lodging.

The canon not only took Abelard into his home, but he gave him complete custody of Heloise's education and moral upbringing. The scholar was to devote as much of his leisure time as he deemed necessary to advance Heloise's education. Still thinking Heloise a child, Fulbert even authorized Abelard to chastise her physically if he found her idle in her studies.

Not long thereafter master and pupil became lovers. Aristotle and the reading of the Holy

Writ had little meaning now. "I thought of nought but Heloise, everything brought her image to mind."[16] Nothing mattered but their new-found passion. Abelard remembered these hours well, "tender words instead of literature and hands that sought each other rather than the pages of books."[17] By day, philosophical discussions became excuses for the increasing frequency of their meetings. To allay suspicion and maintain the appearance of normalcy, Abelard would treat Heloise sternly and would often feign extra harshness in the presence of servants. By night, however, after the uncle and his domestics had retired, the two lovers met at a secluded spot in the house described by Abelard as one in which we had "no lions to fear."[18] It was during these nocturnal hours that they experienced the joy of utter abandonment to love and left no desires unfulfilled. (At least that is what their letters seem to imply.)

Although she made no reference to it, Heloise had been overwhelmed when she first met the renowned master. We can only guess to what extent her response was fuelled by Abelard's fame or Abelard the man. There is no doubt, however, that she was passionately in love and that her surrender was complete. In one of her letters, written years after their fateful meeting, Heloise corroborates that, from the very beginning, she had been ready to carry out her teacher's every wish.

As for the scholar, it was not quite the same. There was at first no hint of romance; his motivation, he told us afterwards, was "lust and conceit."[19] But it was not long before the seducer was himself ensnared by the trap he had so carefully laid for Heloise. Abelard had been conquered by the very passion which had made his young pupil such easy prey. "Countless moments of tenderness, feelings surpassing anything I had heretofore thought possible,"[20] these words disclose the change which had taken place in him and unmistakably reveal the depth of his involvement. It comes as no surprise then, Abelard began to neglect his commitments. His interest in school and students faded and the study of philosophy lost its luster. Inspired by the Muse he exalted Heloise in poetry and song, and before long the city was aflame with the melodies and verses he had composed for her. Every street, every house resounded with her name, all Paris caught the echo.

Months passed, but the obvious continued to elude the canon. His initial confidence in Abelard remained unshaken. As far as Fulbert knew, the scholar's reputation had been without a blemish and, perhaps reluctant to view his niece with suspicion, he rejected what allusions might have reached his ears as jealous fabrications. Trying later to account for Fulbert's apparent blindness, Abelard referred to St. Jerome, who had said that it was quite common for a man to be unaware of what transpires in his home and that often he will remain ignorant of his wife's infidelities or his children's indiscretions, long after they've become the talk of the town.

Rumors persisted, however, and in order to eradicate them and clear the names of his niece and her distinguished master, Fulbert decided to investigate the malicious talk. One evening the canon had Abelard followed. Later that night he himself surprised his niece and her tutor in a most compromising embrace. The shock almost killed the furious Fulbert. To escape the canon's wrath, Abelard fled the house at once, but only to move into lodgings nearby.

35

Thereafter Fulbert strictly forbade all contact between Heloise and her tutor and made it almost impossible for anyone to approach her. The lovers bore the sudden parting with difficulty. As the weeks passed, worries about Heloise's well-being haunted Abelard. When one of his messages finally succeeded in reaching her, Heloise replied by exultantly informing him that she was carrying his child.

He at once made arrangements for her escape. On a set night, when Fulbert was scheduled to be elsewhere, Heloise left her uncle's house and fled with Abelard to Brittany. In spite of the hazards of travel through medieval France, they made their way unscathed to the home of Abelard's sister in Le Pallet. Abelard gives us no details of their journey, saying only that Heloise travelled disguised as a nun. They were warmly received by his family and it was here in Brittany that Heloise gave birth to a son, to whom she gave the unusual name of Astrolabe.[21]

There is no record of how long Abelard remained in Le Pallet after the birth of their son, but we do know that he was eager to resume his position as the head of the schools of Paris.

To return with Heloise as his mistress was unthinkable: new scandals would be inevitable and Fulbert would not sit idly by while Abelard's treachery went unpunished. Unable to endure the thought of separation, Abelard decided to effect a reconciliation with Fulbert. As long as Heloise remained in the care of his family, he had little to fear by meeting face to face with her uncle. The canon was unlikely to harm him or have him assassinated; the danger of reprisal against Heloise was too obvious, considering that an eye for an eye was a fully accepted concept of justice in those days.

Abelard returned to Paris, met with the canon and offered to marry Heloise on the condition that, for the sake of his career, the union not be made public. Extraordinary as it may seem, the scholar saw no self-serving motive in his efforts to reconcile with Fulbert. Quite the opposite, he tells us it was out of "compassion for the old man's anxieties"[22] that he approached him with his proposal of a secret marriage. Fulbert, surprised at the sudden turn of events, accepted the offer, consented to honor Abelard's request for silence and "sealed the agreement with an embrace."[23]

37

Back in Brittany, when Abelard informed
Heloise of these developments, she immediately
raised objections. Besides strongly disapprov-
ing of their proposed return to Paris, she wanted
no marriage, secret or otherwise. She did not
believe that her uncle would be appeased by
such an arrangement or that their union would
remain secret. Most of all, Heloise feared that
their return to Paris would endanger Abelard's
life.

There were other considerations for her
opposition to a wedded state, just as personal
and as compelling: matrimony, in 12th-century
Christian France, constituted a considerable
lowering of status for a teacher or a cleric. If
such an individual were to forgo celibacy, he
would be judged guilty of moral degradation,
of falling away from scholarship.

Heloise realized that although Abelard proposed marriage, it was not matrimony he sought.
To be sure, he wanted her—but he wanted her
for the purpose of venting his carnal passion
and he wanted the marriage only to ensure his
having and holding her. She recognized that
matrimony would be of no advantage to the
man she loved, that it would give him no benefit

he did not already have. On the contrary, the wedded state would only serve to destroy his reputation and his chances for advancement. But beyond that, and of no minor importance to her, it would irrevocably blemish his fame in which she gloried, for it would deny him a place among the illustrious philosophers of the world.

To dissuade Abelard from what she later referred to as the ill-fated wedlock, Heloise used ingenious arguments: destiny had made him belong to the world and it would be a great loss were he—who was created for the benefit of all—to devote himself to one woman only; that the cries of children and the cares of a family were utterly incompatible with the tranquillity and application which a life of study required. Continuing, she reminded Abelard of the ideals he himself had expounded, of the counsel of Seneca, the Roman teacher whom he had so consistently quoted and of the exhortations of Paul. All were of one mind: that the single, or unmarried state, was inseparable from the true cleric or the true philosopher. Reinforcing her argument, Heloise recalled the fate of Socrates: his stormy life with Xanthippe and the notoriety of their marital battles, still sending their cautionary signals around the world. Further asserting the disadvantages of married life, Heloise confronted Abelard with Theophrastus, to whose unkind dissertations on marriage he had first introduced her. The Greek philosopher held that wise men refrain from wedlock because it is impossible to know the kind of wife one gets until after one is locked in the state of matrimony. Moreover, Theophrastus believed it burdensome to be married to a poor woman and an even greater burden to keep a rich one content. He also felt that if one's wife were beautiful, men would pursue her; if, on the other hand, she were an ugly woman, she might do the pursuing. One either had to keep a watchful eye on the object of everyone's desire, or one would have to be content with a woman no one wanted. "Take no wife," he admonished, "hire a good servant instead!"

In her final plea, Heloise beseeched Abelard to shun marriage and maintain the privilege of a cleric; or, if he chose not to heed the classic view, he should uphold the dignity of a philosopher and remain free. As for herself, she felt purer sharing her love with him as heretofore, and she called God to witness that it was sweeter and more meaningful to be tied to Abelard by bonds of affection rather than by the compulsion of marriage vows.

By marrying the scholar, Heloise felt she would vilify herself as well, if for no other reason than for having given her consent, without which there could be no marriage. In the eyes of the world, unfair as she perceived it to be, she would stand accused and be held accountable for whatever might ensue. People would say she had sought matrimony for her own advancement and that her surrender to Abelard was but a means to further that end, when, in actuality, she had opposed such a commitment with all the might she could muster. It is not inconceivable that she might have wanted marriage for herself, but it is indisputable that she did not want it for the philosopher, not at the price he would have to pay for what she considered unabashed folly.

Apparently Denise had also cautioned her brother on the pitfalls of married life. In an eighteenth-century translation of the correspondence, whose authenticity, however, is not verifiable, she tells Abelard that a learned wife was not always more amiable, nor that the qualities a man desired in a mistress were necessarily those he sought in a wife. Marriage, she warns, could well become a tomb of love instead of the blissful happiness it was meant to be: "when her attractive features have waned and she has lost her charms, would he not regret?"

Abelard remained unyielding and Heloise, having exhausted all possible arguments, was no longer able to refuse marriage. Not wishing to "offend so deeply"[24] the man she loved, she saw no alternative but to let Abelard's will prevail and to let fate take its course.

With a strange premonition about Fulbert's apparent change of heart, Heloise left her infant son with Denise and her family and returned with Abelard to Paris. They were joined in holy wedlock a few days after their arrival, having spent the preceding night in the customary prayer vigil. (The name of the chapel and its location in the old city remain unknown.) The ceremony was performed at dawn, attended by only a few friends as well as Fulbert and some of his servants, upon whose presence the canon had insisted.

Abelard's mind was finally at peace. He was confident that his marriage to Heloise had pacified the canon and that henceforth there was no need for apprehension. Nevertheless, the next few months were not happy ones. In order to keep their marriage concealed, Heloise was again living in her uncle's house and her meetings with Abelard were rare and clandestine.

Fulbert had meanwhile begun to divulge that the celebrated philosopher and his niece were husband and wife. Clearly, the canon had never intended to keep the marriage secret. The presence of members of his household at the nuptials could have had but one purpose: to forestall any later denials that the wedding had taken place. Understandably, the canon was more interested in protecting his own reputation than in shielding Abelard's career; but in all fairness to Fulbert, the seduction of Heloise had been common knowledge, and matrimony was small reparation for so scandalous an offense. Were he unable to publicize the espousal,

43

neither the honor of his niece nor his own good
name would be recovered.

As news of their marriage spread, Abelard's
concern increased. Heloise, to protect her husband and counter repeated inquiries, swore
sacred oaths, disclaiming their nuptial bond.
Incensed by these denials, Fulbert made life
increasingly difficult for his niece. There ensued
such stormy scenes and physical abuses that
once again Abelard had to remove Heloise from
her uncle's house. This time she sought shelter
at Argenteuil, in the very convent where she
had spent her early years. To authenticate her
presence here, Abelard informs us he had her
"dressed in a nun's garb."[25] To all appearances
Heloise had entered a convent: her marital
status could no longer be questioned, for she
could not be married to the philosopher and at
the same time be confessed in a nunnery.

Abelard, however, could not stay away and
visited his wife frequently at Argenteuil. The
aura of their surroundings appeared not to have
disturbed the philosopher, nor had it dimmed
his ardor. Years afterward he still remembered
the nights in the refectory, where he had in-
temperately imposed his will on her, and in one

of his letters remorsefully reminded Heloise of those passionate encounters, when neither holy days nor the proximity of sacred images could deter him from venting his unbridled lust.

When Fulbert eventually learned of his niece's whereabouts, "he became enraged beyond control."[26] He felt the scholar had again betrayed him, just as he had done when, as Heloise's tutor, he so blatantly dishonored her under the canon's own roof, the incident which had made Fulbert the laughing stock of Paris. As the irony of fate would have it, the uncle, for whom the disguise was least intended, came to accept the deception unquestioningly. Fulbert was convinced that Abelard had tired of Heloise and that her retirement to the convent was an opportune means for the philosopher to dissolve the marriage.

The events of the vengeful attack which followed are well known. Fulbert's hirelings, having gained entry to Abelard's quarters by bribing his servant, surprised the scholar in his sleep and brutally mutilated him. It was a terrible tragedy. All France was horrified by Fulbert's reprisal. The next few days saw Paris in an uproar. Women wept openly as raging crowds of students and streams of sympathizers swarmed through the streets and assembled outside Abelard's lodgings. But instead of bringing him comfort, their cries of outrage only heightened his awareness of the barbarity to which he had been subjected. Ultimately, Abelard suffered more from the sympathy of his wailing followers than from his bodily wounds. "The pain," he complained, "seemed insignificant now, compared to the intolerable shame I felt at being emasculated!"[27] Much later, long after his religious transformation, he was to describe the assault as just retribution for his treachery: "God had punished that part of my body with which I had committed my sins and used Fulbert, whom I had betrayed, as His avenger."[28]

Miraculously, Abelard lived; but the ordeal left him in complete confusion. How could he face his students "without being ridiculed and pointed at by every finger as a monstrous spectacle?"[29] How could he explain the loss of his manhood, when even the Bible had rejected eunuchs, "those cut in the stones,"[30] as unclean creatures, forbidden to enter the House of the Lord? His defeat was complete, his reputation ruined and his enemies jubilant. Ashamed to be seen in public and at a loss as to where to turn, Abelard admitted in time that it was not religious devotion, but his wretched condition, which prompted his decision to retreat to a monastic community to find calm and seclusion.

Still, there was Heloise and the intolerable fear that she could now belong to someone else. Although Abelard's obsessive jealousy was void of all reality, it nevertheless magnified his anxieties to a point of insufferable torment. It was undoubtedly this state of desperation which led him to demand that Heloise retire from the world and become a nun. The sacrifice Abelard had asked of his young wife was cruel in itself, but to insist that she consecrate herself prior to his own entry into monastic life was a demand which one could possibly explain, but it was neither excusable nor would it earn the scholar any laurels. Heloise felt shamed and immeasurably hurt by this want of trust and the scars of that outrage would remain with her all her life.

In his autobiography Abelard revealed that he had lived in fearful doubt of the firmness of her commitment until Heloise had been form-

47

ally consecrated. He described the scene in the chapel of Argenteuil, where friends and bystanders had milled around Heloise and, because of her youth and the heavy yoke of convent life, attempted to dissuade her from taking her vows. To no avail—she motioned them aside and stepped forward. But there were no invocations on her lips, instead of Christian prayers her thoughts went to a pagan, the Roman playwright Lucan, with whose works they were both familiar. In his epic poem "Pharsalia" his heroine Cornelia, consumed by sorrow and blaming herself for her husband's ruination, followed him into death. It was part of Cornelia's soliloquy,[31] her despairing farewell to the world before committing suicide, which Heloise recited as she hurried to the altar. With tears in her eyes, but without a moment's hesitation, she took the veil the Bishop had blessed and embraced the life of a religious.

Obviously, Heloise's consecration was not brought about by religious inspiration or by her love of God, nor was her entry into a cloister prompted by the desire to repent for her sins. Far from it! Heloise donned a nun's

habit for the love of a man. She submitted to
the severity of cloistral life to atone to Abelard
for the terrible crime she had committed against
him by accepting marriage, knowing she should
have remained steadfast in her refusal. It was
this offense for which she could find no excuse
and of which she could not absolve herself.
Though it was Abelard who had disregarded
her feelings and turned a deaf ear to her counsel, who had thrust her from one untenable
situation into another and who, in fact, had
devastated her life, it was Heloise who never
ceased to castigate herself for having been the
cause of his calamity. She held fast to that
premise and we have no reason to believe these
were not her true sentiments.

What a relief for the scholar to know Heloise
confined within the sanctity of a cloister. And
yet he was astonished that a young woman, who
loved life so well, would so readily renounce
all that was dear to her. How little did he know
her! How small was his perception of the infinite depth of her feelings! Heloise was, at this
time, still in her teens!

As had been his intention, Abelard entered
the Royal Abbey of St. Denis, one of the wealth-

iest and most renowned monasteries in France. Kings and nobles received their education there and the steady flow of prominent visitors provided the abbey with an endless array of entertaining diversions. Rules at the Royal Abbey, like those in many other monasteries of that period, were only loosely enforced and discipline was accordingly lax. As for the monks of St. Denis, it is said they "scarcely exhibited even the appearance of religion,"[32] and their holiday festivities rivalled in gaiety the merrymaking held in any castle in France. Founded by King Dagobert in the seventh century, the abbey lay on the banks of the Seine, not far from Paris. It was also not far from Argenteuil, a fact Heloise must have borne well in mind when she so readily agreed to join the Sisters there. That Abelard might not always remain at nearby St. Denis, or the possibility of the complete separation which later took place, would never have occurred to her, not in her wildest imaginings.

When Abelard arrived at his new home at St. Denis, his wounds were scarcely healed. At the urging of his abbot and the clerics, he returned to his writing and, in keeping with his new responsibilities, taught the Scriptures to the poor. "It was for the sake of God now," he wrote, "and not as before, for riches and fame."[33] Conditions at the abbey, however, were not what he expected to find at a monastery. Instead of solitude and quiet seclusion, he found "lewdness and debauchery. It was all-pervasive," he reported, "beginning with the lowliest friar and extending to the abbot himself."[34]

There remains little doubt, Abelard had seriously misjudged the situation by seeking tranquillity in so wordly a retreat as the Royal Abbey. The monks, for their part, had erred by expecting the Abelard of old. They had known him as a vibrant troubador, the lover of Heloise, whose wit and brilliance would further enhance the good life in their abbey. Instead, they had a morbid and stern disciplinarian in their midst, an ascetic monk whose bitter reprimands never ceased. Unwilling to tolerate the atmosphere which he found, Abelard began to assail the friars' way of life and publicly denounce them for their intolerable depravity. Such criticism was not kindly received from a friar who could so easily forget his own past, particularly from one who, until he lost his manhood, had practiced no self-restraint of any kind and whose motivation for entry into monastic life was, at best, questionable. As with everything he undertook, Abelard knew no half-measures. Soon he had become more saintly than the saints and his newly acquired religious fervor alienated his fellow-monks, who, before much time had elapsed, came to resent his presence.

Abelard eventually left the abbey for Maison-celle, a village near Provins, where he settled in one of the priories belonging to St. Denis. According to a contemporary profile, these priories were estates and country-houses, of which the abbey had a great many. In the process of securing a place in the Hereafter, "some dying sinner would attempt to corrupt the Supreme Judge by donating to the monks of the abbey a chateau or a farm with its cattle, all its men and women and other commodities of value."[35] These properties were eventually converted into smaller units, from which the abbey derived a sizable part of its wealth.

It was never clear if Abelard's departure from St. Denis was voluntary or whether he had been "urged" to leave and live elsewhere. The general belief is that Abbot Adam had been forced to relieve the monastery of the consistently irksome friar.

Although Abelard was committed to teach the Scriptures in his new quarters, he began to intersperse his lessons with secular rhetoric. His purpose, he tells us, was to use these seminars as bait to lure his students into the study of the Holy Writ. As in the past, his lectures attracted large throngs of pupils. A writer of the time related that the surge of followers was such that the facilities in the district sufficed neither to house them nor to feed them.

The migration of students to Maisoncelle, however, provoked the hostility of Abelard's rivals in the region. The chief instigators of the renewed attempt to silence him were Lotulf of Lombardy and Alberic of Rheims, two aggressive antagonists whose quarrels dated back to their student days in Anselm's academy. Time, apparently, had not diminished their enmity, in fact, they had now become Abelard's most rancorous opponents. The point of dispute was, apart from their ecclesiastical differences, the proximity of Abelard's new learning center to their schools. These two prominent headmasters had lost large numbers of pupils to the Breton and the loss of income must have been considerable. They at once began to denounce him, "lodging complaints with abbots and bishops, wherever influential ears would listen, that occupying quarters outside one's monastery and teaching secular literature usurped Church authority and was contrary to monastic practice."[36] Further, on the basis of some of his writings, they accused him of impiety and heresy.

In time their efforts and intrigues gained their objective and led to the scholar's tragic condemnation before the Council of Soissons in 1121. Abelard vehemently denied the charges and accused his opponents of fraud and of deliberately distorting the meaning of his words. Nevertheless, the Council censored his treatise on the Trinity, on the flimsy grounds that he had issued it without the Church's authorization, and decreed that this text was to be burned. Compounding Abelard's humiliation, he was forced to commit his work to the flames with his own hands.

As an adjunct to his punishment, the scholar

54

was forbidden to return to his community at Maisoncelle, and he was treated as if he were a convicted heretic. As such, he was assigned to St. Medard near Soissons, a monastery which served as a penitentiary and reform school. "It was equipped with a well-appointed ascetical armory, better known as a whipping-room. To it were sent," so a portrayal of the period relates, "the ignorant to be instructed, the depraved to be corrected and the obstinate to be tamed."[37] But the abbot of St. Medard, Geoffrey of the Stag's-neck, who had witnessed the spectacle of Abelard's trial, was aware of the mockery of justice which had been perpetrated, and treated Abelard more as a guest at his abbey than a prisoner.

Abelard's confinement lasted several months. When the irregularities of the Council's proceedings became known, there followed an outburst of indignation. Now that the judges were to be judged and their turn to defend themselves had come, a rash of reciprocal incriminations ensued among the persecutors themselves. Even Lotulf and Alberic downgraded their participation in the affair and tried to extricate themselves by casting blame on others. As a result of all of this, the order of imprisonment was annulled and Abelard was granted permission to return to St. Denis. The monks and their abbot, however, had not forgotten the scholar's devastating criticism of their community, and it soon became apparent that they did not welcome Abelard's renewed presence among them.

The inevitable came to pass. An apparently innocent remark by Abelard, questioning the true identity of their abbey's Patron Saint (who was the Patron of France as well), gave Abbot Adam the opportunity he had been seeking. He convened his council and, with a vilifying tirade against the scholar, accused him of slander. Following the Abbot's lead, the assembly unanimously declared Abelard's utterance an affront to the glory of their monastery and an insult against France. The scholar was thrown into the abbey dungeon, to be kept there until he could be turned over to the King's court for trial. Abelard managed to escape and fled to the priory of St. Ayoul in the neighboring territory of Count Theobald. The Count appears to have been a friend by whom he had been welcomed and sheltered on previous occasions.

Shortly thereafter, in February 1122, Abbot

56

Adam died unexpectedly, and the King's close friend and advisor, Suger, became the new abbot of St. Denis. The altered circumstances brought relief from immediate pressures and Abelard's situation improved. Once again his connection to the Court proved to be expedient. The prominent royal seneschal, Etienne de Garlande, intervened on his behalf. As a result, Abelard was declared free, given permission to continue his life as a monk and to move to any retreat of his choosing. In order not to jeopardize the prestige of St. Denis, however, he was not permitted to place himself under the jurisdiction of any other monastery which might benefit by his scholastic renown, nor was he allowed to take up residence with secular or nonmonastic friends.

Accordingly, he withdrew to a parcel of land the Duke of Brittany had given him during an earlier visit. It was an isolated and sparsely populated spot bordered by the Ardusson River, some twelve miles from Troyes, in the vicinity of Nogent-sur-Seine. Heloise said that when Abelard first arrived in that part of the valley, it had been the haunt of robbers and the home of wild boars. At the water's edge, he and a

57

clerk who had accompanied him built their huts and a small oratory-like structure, "rudely fashioned from branches of trees and reeds from the river, and daubed over with mud."[38] There, Abelard told us, far removed from everything, they lived like hermits hiding in the wilderness; but their solitude was short-lived. Once his whereabouts became known, a number of his former pupils joined their impoverished teacher in his new retreat. Too weak to work with his hands and too proud to beg, Abelard returned to what he knew best: he began to instruct again. In exchange for his lectures, his students provided food and all else needed for his sustenance.

As time went on, word spread through Europe's academic centers that Abelard had resumed his lectures. It was as though a dike had broken—students, by the hundreds, gathered their belongings and descended upon the peaceful forest near Nogent. Rich and poor alike left their towns and villages to build their shelters near Abelard's. We are told they endured all sorts of hardships, slept on mats of straw, ate roots and coarse peasant bread and drank water from the river. The comfort of their homes, their sumptuous meals, wines and pretty maidens were left behind. The fascination Abelard had held for them had not waned and his lectures were as compelling as ever. When the oratory had grown too small, his followers built a sturdier and larger structure, "one of timber and stone."[39]

Abelard spent three fulfilling years in his new-found haven. In the brightness of the valley and the pleasant climate of the region he had at last gained some semblance of peace. For that reason, he told us, he had named the oratory The Paraclete, meaning comfort and consolation, and it was out of gratitude that he had dedicated the station to his Comforter.

But there was one enemy, he recalled, "the echo"[40]: the echo of his popularity, which had reached the ears of his detractors. Envious of his renewed triumph, they began yet another campaign of harassment. Alberic and Lutolf once again took up their slanderous game by inciting others, bringing Abelard more enemies, notably the fierce Abbot Bernard of Clairvaux, founder of the Cistercian order. The new attack rested on the assertion that in Abelard's dedication of The Paraclete, he had dignified but

59

one of the entities of the Trinity. Inasmuch as this deviated from the teachings of the Church, they accused the scholar of offending Christian faith and negated the lawfulness of so sanctifying the oratory. The tranquillity of The Paraclete was shattered. Terrified by the power of his new adversaries and frightened by visions of another Council of Soissons with its perfidious accusations, he hastily abandoned The Paraclete. In a telling indictment in his autobiography Abelard relates that he was "ready to flee Christian lands," and was about to seek refuge among the Moors in Arab Spain, where, along with scholarship and a love of the arts, religious tolerance flourished.

He set that project aside, however, when he received an invitation from the monks of St. Gildas of Rhuys to become their shepherd. Their abbot had died and the monks had unanimously chosen Abelard to replace him. The monastery of St. Gildas was situated in a remote corner on the coast of Brittany, far removed from his persecutors. Interested in putting distance between himself and his detractors, and eager for a position of authority, he accepted the call. The Duke of Brittany, whose concurrence was required, agreed to Abelard's installation at St. Gildas, and when Suger raised no objection, the scholar journeyed to his new destination without further ado.

Conditions at St. Gildas, however, turned out to be by far the most intolerable of any that Abelard endured. It appears that his problems began soon after his arrival in 1128: "I was named abbot of St. Gildas, where I now live and suffer daily harassments. I find myself in a wild country, whose population is unrestrained and whose language I do not understand. My conversations are with the rudest of people and my walks are along the inaccessible shore of a raging sea."[41] These words cryptically point to an unhappy and precarious situation. To be sure, the monks at St. Gildas were a primitive and undisciplined lot, whose dialect was totally unintelligible to an outsider's ear. They ignored their monastic rules and lived openly with their concubines and offspring. Each one was responsible for his own sustenance and had to provide for himself and his family out of his own pocket. We must bear in mind that these monks had clamored for Abelard's leadership in the mistaken belief that his

61

fame and influence would bring them relief from their wretched existence. Somewhat earlier, a neighboring lord had appropriated much of their abbey's property and imposed heavy levies on what was left of their land. Consequently, the entire community at St. Gildas suffered great hardships. On occasion, when their food supplies ran low, the brothers would roam the countryside and beg, borrow or steal whatever was not tightly secured.

Abelard appeared to have been unaware of the prevailing conditions. No sooner did he set about to bring reforms and spiritual guidance into the lives of the monks than they began their resistance. Instead of the spiritual affirmations he meted out to them, they wanted him to exert his authority and use his verbal skills to intercede with their neighboring tyrant, to fight for their rights and procure more food for their table. Abelard did what he could, but his intervention with the hostile neighbor only served to increase the tyrant's animosity towards the monks and turn the main thrust of his ill will against Abelard himself. Later, in an attempt to help his impoverished sons, Abelard delved into his own purse, but after his resources were exhausted, the more malcontent among them openly defied his authority. It was obvious, Abelard's presence at the monastery did not bring about the benefits the monks had expected when they summoned him to St. Gildas.

But to return to Heloise. She had, meanwhile, remained at Argenteuil. Of her eight or nine forlorn years there we know only that she was well-loved and had just been named Prioress, when adversity struck again. Suger, to prove his worth as the new Abbot of St. Denis, had begun to reorganize his monastery. In the process he found documents relative to the history of the nearby cloister, revealing that it had belonged to St. Denis in earlier times. Utilizing his considerable influence with King Louis VI, he opportunely brought to light "licentious behavior"[42] among the nuns at Argenteuil.

There followed an inquiry led by the bishops who apparently had become convinced of the corruption within the convent. Under the pretense of restoring a more pious community, Abbot Suger reclaimed Argenteuil for St. Denis and took possession of the nunnery. Heloise and her sisterhood were to be expelled. On re-examination of the affair in later years, there remained no doubt that conditions at Argenteuil had been lax, but no more so than those prevailing in other cloisters of that time. In other words, the charges against the nuns had been exaggerated simply to give Suger good reason to seize the institution.

By the time the news of Heloise's impending eviction reached Abelard, most of the nuns had relocated to the Convent of St. Mary of Footel near Champigny, where Suger had directed them. Heloise, with some of her companions, however, had stayed behind. Abelard never mentioned the incident and since Heloise chose to remain silent on the subject, we will never know why they refused to join their sisters at their new location: was it in protest of their expulsion? Or did they have misgivings regarding the moral attitude of a few renegades within their sisterhood, and was this the reason for their refusal?

Whatever the case may have been, Abelard hurried back to The Paraclete which had lain idle from the time he had abandoned it three years before. Ever since then he had been plagued by the thought that his oratory was unattended, and that a place of worship in disuse would be offensive to God. Hence, as the legal holder of the property, he made the necessary arrangements and placed The Paraclete at the disposal of the homeless Heloise and her flock. From now on the sanctuary could redeem its name and give renewed comfort to those in need.

We know nothing of the Sisters' arrival, nor are any particulars available of Abelard's encounter with his wife after their long separation. Whenever he visited The Paraclete, however, he avoided being alone with her and would not even remain in her close proximity, unless members of her community were present. On those occasions when he did see her, he was careful to conduct himself in an impersonal and businesslike manner and at no time, to her dismay, did he betray the slightest personal interest in her.

As might have been expected, the years of neglect and the ravages of time had taken their toll of The Paraclete; nevertheless the land and buildings gave the new arrivals a home of sorts and a place to worship. Eventually, after the cabins had been restored and the oratory put in order, the Bishop of Troyes gave Abelard permission to establish a religious community under Heloise's supervision. In November 1131 Innocent II confirmed the endowment in a Papal Bull.

In monastic environments hard labor had an intrinsic value: the more difficult the task, the greater the reward from Heaven. Generally, people from the surrounding settlements would eagerly lend assistance, clear stony fields and cultivate steep hills, turning arid land into fertile soil. And so it appears to have been at The Paraclete. It was a difficult beginning. Extreme poverty and deprivations scarred the small community, but once their plight became known, helping hands started to reach them from all corners of the land. "Before long, Heloise had won the affection of many," Abelard recounted. "The bishops came to love her as a daughter, the abbots as their sister and the laity as their mother; all of them marvelled at her prudence and at her incomparable gentleness and compassion."[43] Prelates and nobles contributed generously to the young community and, from all indications, conditions at The

Paraclete improved rapidly. According to Abelard, Heloise's future seemed to be assured. He believed that she had accomplished more in a short period than he could have done for her and her Sisters in a lifetime.

Abelard's stay near The Paraclete, however, had given rise to ugly rumors and insinuations. At first neighbors had chided him for not doing more for the Sisters, either by comforting them with his presence, or by calling attention, throughout the region, to their plight. But when his visits to The Paraclete grew increasingly frequent and were of longer duration, they accused him of still harboring a carnal interest in the woman he had once loved. With his enemies ever eager to exploit the slightest opportunity to defame him, his continued visibility at The Paraclete might not only jeopardize the very existence of Heloise and her flock, but could become a threat to his own precarious situation. It must have been at this juncture that Abelard made his decision to leave the area and secretly returned to St. Gildas.

The separation was tragic for Heloise, all the more so since it is doubtful whether she understood the true motive for Abelard's withdrawal.

If she did, she never appreciated it—and this at a time when his intentions appear to have been beyond reproach.

Back in St. Gildas, Abelard found the situation had in no way improved. His sons, he wrote, were now a greater menace to his life than his avowed enemies. First they tried to end his rule by poisoning his food. When that, because of his constant vigilance, came to naught, they put a deadly potion into his chalice at the altar. That failing, poison found its way into his food again, when, accompanied by a group of monks, he visited his brother Dagobert at Nantes. Here, amidst his family, his enemies thought he would be less on his guard. But instead of Abelard falling victim, it was one of his companions who paid with his life. By a quirk of fate the unfortunate friar ate a dish prepared for Abelard and died on the spot. After that incident, Abelard left the abbey for a time, but remained in the vicinity, moving from one abode to another in order to create confusion as to his whereabouts. The monks responded by hiring assassins who would lie in wait for him along the roads Abelard was expected to travel. Still, he managed to thwart their efforts and stay alive.

But now fate dealt Abelard another blow: on one of his journeys through the countryside his horse threw him and he broke a vertebra in his neck. Abelard told us he was in great pain and more debilitated by that fall than by the vengeful assault he had suffered at the hands of Fulbert's henchmen. This notwithstanding, he was determined to curb his rebellious congregation and proceeded to excommunicate the monks he thought to have been the biggest offenders. Soon he realized, however, that those who remained at the abbey were worse than the ones he had banished. Not even the Papal Legate, whom Abelard had summoned, could restore order. And so the lawlessness of his wretched sons continued and Abelard's days turned into a constant struggle to protect himself from their violent impulses.

Almost thirteen years were to pass before Abelard was heard from again. Then a letter he had written to a friend, most likely a brother-monk, came into Heloise's possession. We may even assume it was this very friend who had directed the communication into her hands. The letter was a reply in which Abelard showed the monk's problems to be minor in comparison to his own tribulations and gave a detailed account of his life as an example of fate's cruelty. When Heloise read the sorrowful narrative, written in the hand of the man she loved above all else on earth, her long-suppressed feelings for him flared anew. She realized that Abelard had found neither the peace nor the tranquillity he had sought in monastic life.

In her memory she relived the past, the happiness which his presence during those few short years had given her, and the unending sorrows which followed. Out of these remembrances, fused with the terrible anguish of having been forsaken, Heloise began her first letter.

F I R S T L E T T E R

BELOVED ABELARD: Some time ago a letter you had written to a friend happened to fall into my possession. I recognized your handwriting the very instant I saw it and my heart trembled as I broke the seal of a dispatch not addressed to me. Though I knew better, I had no scruples in breaking the rules of good breeding when I was to hear news of one who means so much to me.

But dear did my curiosity cost me! What turmoil it caused within me to find the whole letter filled with gall and wormwood! I met with my name many times; never did I see it without feeling apprehension about what might follow. What reflections did I not make! I began to consider the past anew and felt myself oppressed with memories; yes, thinking of our bygone days is as painful now as when I first began to feel my grief. Alas, a cruel uncle and a wounded lover will always be present in my aching heart!

Nothing can ever blot from my mind the rancorous malice of your opponents Alberic and Lotulf, nor what you have endured in defense of your writings; neither shall I forget the envy your success raised against you. I shall always carry with me the memory of your hard-earned reputation torn to pieces by the unscrupulous cruelty of pseudo-pretenders to science.

Was not your treatise of divinity condemned to be burned? Were you not threatened with life imprisonment? In vain you maintained in your defense that your enemies imposed upon you opinions quite different from your meanings; it was to no avail that you refuted those deliberate misrepresentations—still, they declared you guilty! With what monstrous accusations had those two false prophets come forth; and how severely they spoke against you before the Council of Soissons! What distortions were invented when the name of The Paraclete was given to your oratory! What a storm was raised against you by the treacherous monks of St. Denis when you did them the honor to be called their brother! And even now your life is in mortal danger at the hands of those whom you call your sons!

The many incidents you described in your letter were told in so moving a manner that one would have had to be callous indeed not to have shed a tear. I must admit I was much easier in my mind before I read your letter. Now I reproach myself for having waited so long before baring my anguish. Permit me for ever to meditate on your calamities; if possible, let me proclaim them throughout the world, to shame an age that has not known how to value you. Your enemies, still full of malice, miss no opportunity to degrade you. The passage of time, which disarms the strongest hatred, seems but to have aggravated theirs; and since no one is interested in protecting you, I will defend you, and I shall spare none.

Alas, my memory is constantly filled with bitter remembrances of past evils; are there yet still more to be feared? Shall my husband never be mentioned without tears, shall his dear name never be spoken but with sighs? All of us here live in despair of your life and every day we tremble at the thought of receiving word of your death. I beg you, let us hear from you without delay and tell us all that concerns you, no matter what the tidings may be. Perhaps, by mingling my sighs with yours, I may make your sufferings less, for it is said that sorrows shared are made lighter. Tell me not you will spare me tears; if you wait for an opportunity to write of pleasant things, you will delay writing too long. Destiny seldom smiles upon the virtuous and fortune is so blind that in a crowd, in which there is perhaps but one wise and brave man, it would be too much to expect that he should be singled out.

I beseech you, dear Abelard, let us hear how you fare, and wait not for miracles; they are too scarce and we are too much accustomed to adversities to expect a happy turn. I shall always have this, if you do not object: when I receive a letter from you, I shall know you still remember me. You may recall that you introduced me to Seneca. He seemed so very sensible to this kind of pleasure, that upon opening a letter from Lucilius, he imagined he felt the same delight as when they conversed together. I believe letters have souls; they can speak; they have in them all that force which expresses the feelings of the heart; they have all the fire of our passions and the tenderness and delicacy of speech, sometimes even a boldness of expression far beyond it.

We may write to each other, so innocent a pleasure is not denied us. Let us not, through negligence, lose the only happiness which is left us and the only one, perhaps, which the malice of our enemies can not take from us. I shall read that you are my husband and you shall see me sign myself your wife. In spite of all that has happened in the past, you may be what you please in your letters. I shall in some measure compensate the loss of no longer being with you by the satisfaction which I shall find in your writing. There I shall read your most sacred thoughts and they shall always be with me. So that corresponding may be no trouble to you, write to me spontaneously, without study. I would rather read the dictates of your heart than those of your mind, and since, by revealing our past to your friend you have re-awakened my sorrows, it would not be unreasonable for you to put my heart at ease by showing it some tokens of your past affection.

I do not reproach you for the innocent artifice you used in comforting a person in distress,

75

by comparing his misfortune to another far greater. Charity is ingenious in finding such pious plans—and to be commended for using them. But do you owe nothing more to us than to that friend, be the friendship between you ever so intimate? We are called your sisters; we call ourselves your children, and if it were possible to think of any expression which could signify a closer relation, or imply greater mutual obligations, we should use it. If we could be so ungrateful as not to speak our just acknowledgments to you, these walls would reproach our silence and speak for us. But without leaving it to that, it will always be my pleasure to say you are the founder of this house, that it is wholly your work. You, by having lived here, have given distinction to a region known heretofore only as a hiding place for outlaws. You have in a literal sense made a den of thieves into a house of prayer. These cloisters owe nothing to public charities, nor were our walls raised by collecting alms in the name of Heaven, which some may even call extortion. The God whom we serve sees nothing but innocent riches and harmless votaries, whom you have placed here. Whatever this young vineyard is it owes to you, and it should remain your mission to care for it and improve it. Though our holy renunciation, our vows and our way of life seem to secure us from all temptation, though our walls and gates prohibit all approaches, it is the outside only, the bark of the tree, that is protected from injuries. What about the inner core, the imperceptible contamination spreading within, even to the heart! Unless continuous care is taken to secure it, it could prove fatal to the most promising plantation. Cultivating the Lord's vineyard is a work of no little labor and our plantation is sown with plants which are still very fresh and fragile; great application and diligence are required if they are to flourish.

I know you are not indifferent, yet your labors are not directed towards us; your cares are wasted upon a group of men whose thoughts are only of the flesh and of earthly endeavors. You refuse to hold out your hand to support those on their way to heaven and who, despite their efforts, can scarcely prevent themselves from falling. In vain you fling the pearls of your divine eloquence before swine, when you speak to those who are now under your care; and you neglect those who deem themselves closest to you, who, tender as they are, would follow you blindly to the ends of the earth. Why are such efforts wasted upon the ungrateful, why not bestow some thought upon your sisters?

But why should I entreat you in the name of your children? Is it possible I should fear obtaining anything from you when I ask it in my own name? Must I use prayers other than my own in order to prevail upon you? Can it be criminal for you to have a discourse with me concerning the Scriptures? Why should I be the only one not to reap the benefits of your knowledge? When you write to me you will be writing to your wife, marriage has made such a correspondence lawful and since you can, without the least scandal, satisfy me, why will you not?

When I lost you, dearest, I lost all I loved on this earth and the manner in which it came about makes my grief inconsolable. You are the cause of all my pain, nothing, therefore, can soothe my hurt unless it comes from you. There is little that you need dread, you need not fly to conquer. You may see me and be witness to all my sorrows without incurring any danger, since you can only relieve me with tears and words. If I have put myself into a cloister with reason, persuade me now to stay in it with devotion.

You remember with what joy I passed whole days listening to your discourses; how, when we were apart, I shut myself from everyone to write to you; how uneasy I was until my letter had reached you; what artful management it required to engage messengers. This detail perhaps surprises you and you are in pain for what may follow. But I am no longer ashamed that my desire for you had no bounds, for I have done more than that. I have ill-treated myself to prove my love for you; I came here to ruin myself in a perpetual imprisonment, that I might give you peace of mind. Nothing but virtue, joined to a love perfectly disengaged from the senses, could have produced such effects. Vice never inspires anything like this, vice reduces the body to servitude. When we love pleasures, we love the living and not the dead. We leave off burning with desire for those who can no longer gratify us. This was my cruel Uncle's notion: he measured my virtue by the frailty of my sex, he believed it was the man and not the person I loved, but how wrong he was! I love you more than ever and so revenge myself on him. I shall love you with all the tenderness of my soul till the last moment of my life. If, formerly, my affection for you was not so pure, if in those days both mind and body wanted you, I told you even then that I was more gratified with possessing your heart than with any other happiness. Your manhood was the least I valued in you.

I believed the more I humbled myself for your sake, the more I would please you and the more I walked in your shadow, the less I would infringe upon your fame. God knows it was always you I thought of, I looked for no marriage bond, no dowry, no gifts; I wanted nothing from you but you yourself. Not even my own will did I think of satisfying, nor my desires, only yours. You cannot but be entirely convinced of this by the extreme unwillingness I showed when you proposed marriage. Though I knew that the name of wife is looked upon with approval in our society, the name of mistress had greater charms for me because it was more free. The bonds of matrimony, however honorable, bear with them commitments, and

I was very unwilling to be compelled to for
ever love a man who would perhaps not always
love me. I despised the name of wife, that I
might live happily with that of friend and mistress, and I find by that letter to your friend,
you have not forgotten that delicacy of passion
which loved you always with the utmost tenderness, and yet wished to love you more! You
very justly stated that I considered those public
vows insipid, and that I had left no stone un-
turned in trying to persuade you not to forfeit
your freedom; but you ignored my reasons for
dissuading you from our ill-fated marriage,
why I preferred love over matrimony, freedom
over bondage. If Augustus, the erstwhile ruler
of the earth, had thought me worthy of marriage and forever placed the world at my feet,
I would still prefer to be yours freely, with whatever name you might choose, be it harlot or
whore—if this would not offend you—rather
than to be his wife and called his Empress.
Wealth and pomp are not the charms of love,
neither do they make for a better being, they
do not imply dignity, nor do they command
respect. Riches and power are the result of
fortune; greatness is a matter of merit. True

81

tenderness makes us separate the loved one from all that is material, and, setting aside his position, fortune or employment, makes us consider him solely for himself. To seek in a husband the material advantages of marriage rather than the man himself, is nothing short of selling oneself. As a rule it is the desire for comfort or position, not love, which makes a woman run into the embraces of a man of means. Ambition, and not affection, forms such unions; these partners in marriage, for ever dissatisfied, long for things they imagine missed. The wife sees a man, richer than her own, spending more lavishly on his spouse and a husband may see a woman whose figure is more seductive than his wife's. Their wants occasion regret and regret begets discontent. Soon they part—or else desire to. I believe, indeed, there may be benefits to such arrangements, but I can never think that the way to experience the joys of an affectionate union is by aiming at advantages other than love itself.

If there is anything that may properly be called happiness here on earth, I am convinced it is the union of two persons who love each other with perfect liberty, who are united by inclination and satisfied with each other's merits. Their hearts are full and leave no room for others; they alone enjoy tranquillity because they enjoy contentment.

If I could believe you are as truly persuaded of my merit as I am of yours, I might say there has been a time when we were such a pair. If I could ever have had any doubts about you, your renown alone would have made me decide in your favor. Everywhere, in every land, people clamored to see you. Women openly showed they felt more for you than mere esteem. Your fame, your manner, the vivacity of your mind and the simplicity of your speech gave everything you said a pleasant turn, very different from those scholars who, with all their learning and wit, often lack the wherewithal to win a woman's heart.

With what ease did you compose verses! Every little song, the smallest sketch of anything you made had a thousand beauties capable of making it last as long as there are lovers in the world. Those who come after us will feel freer to love and think themselves less guilty. The songs you wrote for me will be sung to laud others and will enable them to express their feelings with greater poignancy than their own words ever could. What rivalries did your gallantries cause me! How many ladies have I seen declare their longing for you, when, after a casual encounter they had flattered themselves as being the subject of your poems! Others, in envy, have reproached me that I had no charms but what your wit bestowed on me, nor did I have any advantage over them, other than being loved by you. Can you believe, I thought myself peculiarly fortunate in having a lover to whom I was obliged for my charms and took a secret pleasure in being admired by a man, who, when he pleased, could raise his mistress to the heights of a goddess. I was infinitely pleased with your compliments and read with delight all those praises you offered without reflecting how little I deserved them. I believed myself to be as you described, so that I might be more certain of pleasing you.

That time has passed! Now I mourn for my beloved and of all my joyful moments I have nothing but the painful memory that they are gone. Learn, all of you who once viewed my bliss with envious eyes, that he can never again be mine! Let me then ask, who, among you, would change places with me now? I loved him, but my love became his crime and the very cause of his punishment. We were content with each other and we passed our brightest days in tranquil happiness. If that was a crime, it is a crime I am yet fond of, and I have no other regret save that against my will I must now be innocent. But what am I saying? My misfortune was to have a cruel family whose selfish creed destroyed our lives; had they been reasonable, I would now be living quietly at the side of my dear husband. How cruel and merciless they were when, with blind fury, they hired thugs to assault you in your sleep! Where was I— where was your Heloise then? What joy should I have had in defending you! I would have guarded you from violence at the expense of my life!

There is one thing I would like you to tell me, if you can: how soon after I entered this pious profession you had determined for me did you start ignoring my existence? You know that nothing moved me towards that cloister but your disgrace, yet you neither came to see me, nor could you ever find it in your heart to write to me, not even a single word. Let me

85

hear your reason for casting me aside, or permit me to give you my opinion. Was it not the sole thought of carnal pleasure, rather than affection, which engaged you to me? And was it not when the heat of passion vanished that all the love you had proclaimed for me went with it? This, dearest, is not only my conclusion, it is what all the world believes. Unhappily for me, I have no other explanation, much as I may have wanted to find excuses for you. It seems as though my love, by leaving you nothing to wish for, extinguished your desire.

Poor Heloise! Had you wished to remain distant, you could have; but since your heart has been softened and has yielded, since you have devoted and sacrificed yourself, you have fallen into oblivion!

I am convinced by this sad experience that it is natural to avoid those to whom we have been too much obliged and that uncommon generosity causes neglect rather than gratitude. My heart surrendered too soon to gain the esteem of the conqueror; you took it without difficulty and threw it aside with the same ease. But, ungrateful as you are, I shall be no consenting party to this, and though I ought not to retain a wish of my own, I still preserve, deep in my heart, the wish to be loved by you. When I pronounced my vows, I had with me your last letter in which you protested that you were wholly mine and would never live but for me. Therefore you must bear with me and cope with my feelings, which of right belong to you and from which you can be in no way disengaged.

What folly it is to talk this way! I see nothing about me but marks of Deity and I speak of nothing but Man! I am, nevertheless, earnestly desirous to see you, but if you deny me your presence, I will content myself with a few lines of comfort from your hand. This is a small favor to ask of you, a request you can easily grant since you love to write and write with such ease! I ask for none of your dispatches filled with learning and Holy Writ; all I desire is such correspondence as the heart dictates and which the hand cannot transcribe fast enough.

When, in being professed, I engaged myself to live under the laws you had imposed, I vowed no more than to be yours and thus forced myself into this confinement. Only death, then, can make me leave this cloister to which you have condemned me; my ashes shall rest here and wait for yours, so that I may show to the very last my obedience and devotion to you.

Why should I conceal from you the secret of my call? You know it was neither zeal nor religious devotion which brought me here. Your conscience is too faithful a witness to permit you to forget that. Yet here I am and here I will remain; but if you deprive me of your concern, if I lose your affection, what can I hope for? As you well know, there will be no reward from Heaven for me, for it was not for our Lord I had donned my habit—nothing I have done was for Him. Therefore salvation will elude me and I must strive and labor in vain.

Among those who are wedded to God, I am wedded to a man; among the heroic supporters of the Deity, I am torn by human desire. At the head of a religious community, I remain devoted to you alone. What a monster I am! Enlighten me, Oh Lord, for I know not if my despair or Thy will draws these words from me! I am, I confess, a sinner; but one who, far from weeping for her sins, weeps only for the man she loves; far from abhorring her transgressions, longs only to renew them; and who, with a weakness unbecoming her state, pleases herself continually with memories of the past.

Good God! What is all this! I reproach myself for my faults, I accuse you for yours, and to what purpose? How difficult it is to fight for duty against inclination! I know what obligations this veil lays upon me, but I have a greater awareness of the power you have over my heart.

I am possessed by my feelings; love troubles my mind and disorders my will. Sometimes I am swayed by the sentiment of piety which arises within me, the next moment my imagination takes me to all that is amorous and tender. I tell you today what I would not have said to you yesterday. I considered I had made a vow, taken the veil and am, as it were, dead and buried; yet, unexpectedly, there flare up emotions which overwhelm all these thoughts and cloud alike my reason and my religion. You reign in such inward retreats of my soul that I know not where to attack you; when I try to break those ties by which I am bound to you, I only deceive myself, and all my efforts but serve to bind them faster.

I thought to end my letter here, but now I

am complaining against you, I must unload my
heart and tell you all its jealousies and reproaches. Indeed I thought it somewhat hard
when, at the time we consecrated ourselves to
God, you insisted upon my taking my vows
prior to your taking yours. God knows that I
should not have hesitated, not for one instant,
to precede you, or to follow you to the very
gates of Hell, had you commanded it. "Does
Abelard then," said I, "suspect that, like Lot's
wife, I shall look back?" If my youth and sex
might have caused you to fear that I should
return to the world, could not my entire behavior, and this heart which you ought to have
known, banish such ungenerous apprehensions?
Dearest, my heart was not with me, it was with
you, where it still is and if it is not with you,
it is nowhere. Your distrust hurt me! I said
to myself: "There was a time when he could
rely upon my bare word. Does he now want
solemn affirmations to assure himself of me?
What reason have I given him in the whole
course of my life to cause the least suspicion?
I met him at all his assignations and would I
now decline to follow him to the Seats of Holi-
ness? I, who have not refused to be the victim

of pleasure in order to gratify him, can he think I would refuse to be a sacrifice of honor when he desired it?" Has vice such charms to refined natures, that when once we have drunk of the cup of sinners, it is with such difficulty we accept the chalice of saints? Or did you believe yourself more competent to teach vice than virtue, and be more ready to teach the former than the latter?

No, this suspicion would be injurious to us both. Virtue is too beautiful not to be embraced when you reveal her charms, and vice too unsightly not to be deplored when you display her deformities. Yes, when you wished to please, it all seemed right to me—nothing, with you, I felt, was gross or shameful. I am only weak when I am alone and unsupported by you, therefore it is up to you to make me such as you desire. Had you been less sure of me, or had you had any occasion to doubt my fidelity, I am inclined to believe you would have been less negligent. But what is there for you to fear? I have done far too much and now have nothing more to do but to surmount your ingratitude. During our blissful days you might have wondered whether it was pleasure of the flesh or affection which joined me more to you; but the end proves the beginning and the place from which I now write must surely have dispelled all doubt. Even now I love you as much as ever.

If I had loved pleasures, could I not have found means to gratify myself? I was not yet twenty and there were other men in the world, yet I buried myself alive in a nunnery and triumphed over life at an age when I could have enjoyed it to the fullest. It is to you I sacrifice what remains of this transitory beauty; these widowed nights and tedious days, and since you cannot possess them, I take them from you to offer them to Heaven, and so make but a secondary oblation of my heart, my days and my life!

I am aware that I have dwelled too long on this subject; I ought to speak less to you of your misfortunes and of my sacrifices. We tarnish the lustre of our most beautiful actions, when we applaud them ourselves. This is true and yet there is a time when we may with decency commend ourselves; when we have to do with those whom ingratitude has stupefied. Now if you were this sort of person, this would be a reflection on you. But how can you account for your departing from The Paraclete without taking leave and without a word of reassurance to me?

Irresolute as I am, I still love you and yet I know I can hope for nothing. I have renounced life and stripped myself of all that pleased me; but I find I neither have been able to nor can I now renounce you, Abelard!

Though I have lost the man I love, I still preserve my love. Oh Vows! Oh Convent! I have not lost my feelings; nor has the habit I wear turned me into stone. My heart is not hardened by my imprisonment and I am still sensitive to what has touched me, though, alas, I ought not to be. My lot would be lightened if you would explain the advantages of the rigorous rules you have imposed on us; and if you could assure me of your support without breaking the resolves by which you must live, I should find your exercises more acceptable. Retirement and solitude will no longer shake me, if I may know that I still have a place in your memory. A heart which has loved as mine cannot soon be indifferent. We fluctuate long between love and hatred before we can arrive at tranquillity; and we always deceive ourselves with some forlorn hope that we shall not be utterly forgotten.

Yes, Abelard, teach me the maxims of Divine Love! Since you have cast me aside, I would glory in being wedded to Heaven. My heart adores that title and disdains any other; but tell me how this Divine Love is nourished, how it works, how it purifies. I beg you by the shackles with which I am bound here: ease their weight and make them as bearable for me as I would make them, were they yours to suffer! In the past, when you were impelled by carnal passion, all I could hear were your songs proclaiming joy and gladness. Now that we are in the midst of purity, is it not time you should speak to me of this new happiness and teach me everything that might heighten or improve it? Show me the same enthusiasm you did when you sought sinful pleasures with me, and without changing the ardor of our affections, let us change their object! Let us leave our songs and sing hymns; let us have no transports save for God's glory! If you gratify my request, I shall adhere to my religion and no longer profane my duty.

God has his own right over the hearts of

great men, when He pleases to touch them, He ravishes them. Until that moment arrives, think of me. I expect this from you, a thing you cannot refuse! Love me as your mistress, cherish me as your child, your sister or your wife! And remember how dear you are to me, and how hard I strive to blot your image from my mind!

What a profane confession this is! I tremble and my heart revolts against my reason. But these lines must come to an end! With tears I say good bye, beloved, and should you really wish it, then I say farewell to you for ever!

SECOND LETTER

To his beloved sister Heloise from her Brother Abelard!

It is true, since our conversion from our worldly life to God, I have not written a single line to you. It was, I will say, not negligence but rather your brightness and common sense, which led me to believe that you needed neither my comfort nor my guidance. Your having been elevated to Prioress at Argenteuil was further proof that God gave you the ability to carry through and look after those for whom you are responsible.

Would I have imagined that a letter not intended for you would fall into your hands, I should have been more careful not to have inserted anything which might awaken the memory of those bygone days. It is also true, I described a series of unfortunate incidents in that letter; I did so only in order to ease my friend's suffering over a loss he had sustained. If by this well-meaning intention I have disturbed you, I beg you now to dry the tears which my written words caused you to shed.

Vanity has hitherto made me conceal what pains my soul, but now you force from me what I did not want to reveal. Yes, our circumstances have been altered and we must face the realization that no change of our condition can be expected. The past is behind us and nothing remains now but to erase from our minds all remembrances of what had been.

You call me master; undeniably, you were once entrusted to my care. At that time I seriously endeavored to further your education; it cost you your innocence and me my liberty. Your uncle, who was undoubtedly fond of you, became my enemy. He took revenge and you know well what followed.

You tell me that it is only for me you live under that habit which covers you. Why do you profane your vocation with such statements? Why provoke a jealous God with blasphemy? I hoped that after our separation your sentiments would change and God would deliver you from the turmoil within you. I hoped also, when you could no longer see me, your affection for me would remain in your memory without troubling your mind.

You express yourself eloquently in reproaching me for my clandestine departure and for the years of my silence—why do you not spare me the recital of our trysts and your exactness to them? Have I not enough to suffer without bringing such disturbing thoughts to mind?

What great advantage would we have over others, if, by the study of philosophy, we could learn to govern our own desires! We do not realize to what efforts, what relapses and agitations we subject ourselves! And how long we remain lost in this confusion, unable to exert reason to rule our affections!

And yet your heart still burns with that fatal fire you cannot extinguish. How troublesome it is to love, and how valuable is abstinence when we consider our peace of mind! Remember our excesses of passion and think of our distractions; add to that our cares and our grief; then throw these things out of the account and let love have all the remaining tenderness. How little that is! But for such shadows of enjoyment you are unable to resist and cannot now help writing to me! How much simpler it would be if our humble way of life could assure us our salvation! The pleasure of loving is not eradicated from the soul save by extraordinary effort; it has so powerful an advocate in our breasts that it is difficult to overcome in spite of ourselves. Not even the love of God, in its initial stage, can completely annihilate our feelings for a loved one.

God, in order to punish me, forsook me. You, Heloise, are no longer part of the world, you have renounced it! I am a man of the cloth, devoted to solitude! Shall we not take advantage of our position? Would you destroy my piety at this stage? Would you have me forsake the abbey? Should I renounce my vows? I have made them in the presence of God and where shall I fly from His wrath, should I violate them?

Think of me no more as the founder of your institution, nor as a personage of great importance! I am a miserable sinner, prostrate before my Judge, and with my face pressed to the ground I mix my tears with the earth. Can you see me in this position and solicit me to love you? Come, if you think fit, and in your holy habit thrust yourself between God and me and be a wall of separation! Come and force from me those thoughts and vows I owe to God alone!

Let me beseech you by our former ties, withdraw and avoid the wrath of Heaven! I herewith release you from the oaths of our engagements. Be God's wholly, to whom you are appropriated; I will never oppose so pious a design. I would be much relieved in the knowledge that I had lost you in this manner. Make your virtue a spectacle worthy of men and Heaven! Be humble among your children, assiduous in your choir, exact in your discipline and make even your recreation useful!

You entreat me to return to The Paraclete under the guise of devotion—your earnestness on this point gives me an uneasy feeling. If, in this instance, I have misread the meaning of what you intended to convey to me, my own words would blush. The Church is jealous of its honor and commands that her children be induced to practice virtue by virtuous means. To see me no more, to expect nothing of me, to forget me even as an idea, is what Heaven demands of Heloise! To give up and forget someone we love is an exacting penance and the most difficult. The only way to return to God is by disregarding the creature we adored, and adoring the God whom we had neglected. This may appear harsh to you, but it must be done if we are to achieve our end.

Why do you think I pressed you to take your vows before I took mine? At the risk of your loathing me, I shall tell you. I was frantically jealous and regarded all men as potential rivals. To comprehend this you must know that a man's love has far more distrust than it has assurance. I was apprehensive of many things and imagined you so inured to love, that I feared it would not be long before you entered a new engagement. Jealousy can easily visualize the most abhorrent things. I was anxious to make it impossible for me to doubt you. I pleaded with you and did not rest until you were persuaded that propriety demanded your withdrawal from the eyes of the world; that modesty and the nature of our relationship required it and that, after the ruthless revenge taken upon me, you could expect to be secure nowhere but in a convent.

I will do you justice, you were easily persuaded. In my jealousy I secretly rejoiced in your innocent compliance and yet, triumphant as I was, I yielded you to God with an unwilling heart. I sought to hold on to my gift, for I regarded you as such, as long as I could and only gave you to the care of our Heavenly Father in order to keep you out of the reach of other men. I did not persuade you to religion out of any regard for your happiness, but condemned you to it as an enemy would, who destroys what he cannot carry off. And yet you listened to my reasonings with kindness, and sometimes interrupted me with tears, and urged me to acquaint you with the convents I held in such high esteem.

What a comfort I felt in seeing you confined! I was now at ease and satisfied that you had withdrawn and would not return to the world. But still I was doubtful. I imagined women were incapable of steadfast resolutions unless they were bound by vows. I wanted these vows, and Heaven itself, as security. Holy mansions and impenetrable retreats, from what innumerable fears had they freed me! Religion and piety now kept a strict guard round your walls. What a haven of rest this was for a jealous mind! And with what impatience had I pursued it!

To hasten your being professed I had called

on you every day, exhorting you to this sacrifice. I must confess I would have stopped at nothing and if you had foiled my plans, not only would I not have retired, but my shadow would have pursued you everywhere on this earth.

Thanks to God, my fears were unwarranted. I accompanied you to the altar and while you stretched out your hand to touch the sacred cloth, I heard you distinctly pronounce those words that forever separated you from man. Till then I had thought your youth would hinder my design and prompt you to return to your former life. Is it possible to renounce oneself entirely in early untried youth, at an age which claims the utmost liberty?Judging by our encounter, I imagined you both gullible and easily misled. Might not a small temptation, or the discouragement of friends, have changed your mind? I watched your eyes, your every movement, I trembled at everything. You may call such selfish conduct perfidious and foul. Yes, this was my love—it should provoke naught but the utmost contempt!

I should also like you to know that the very instant I was convinced of your complete devotion, I imagined I had no feelings left for you. I thought it was time to leave off giving you signs of my affection and I considered that by your Holy Espousals, you were now entrusted to the care of Heaven and no longer a charge on me as my wife. My jealousy seemed to have vanished. To be sure, when God is the only rival we have nothing to fear and, having more tranquillity than ever before, I even dared to pray to Him to remove you from my sight. But it was not the time to deliver such rash prayers, my faith was wanting and did not warrant their being heard. Despair and necessity were at the root of my behavior and so I offered an insult to Heaven rather than a sacrifice. I bear alike, then, the guilt of your profession and of the passion that preceded it; therefore I must live in self-abasement all the days of my life. Our follies have penetrated into sacred places; our amours have been a scandal to the country. They are publicized and well known. Let France, which has witnessed our undoing, now bear witness to our repentance.

If your vocation be, as you say, my work, deprive me not of the merit of it by your concerns. Tell me that, by an inward retirement, you will be true to the habit which covers you. Without growing severe, learn from your own misery to support those sisters with less forbearance, and if any thoughts too worldly should importune you, fly to the foot of the altar and pray. Blush at the smallest revolt of your senses. Remember that the least thought for any other than God is adultery. No incense can be more agreeable to evil spirits than earthly passion in the heart of a religious. If, during your life your soul has acquired a habit of loving, feel it now no longer save for God, and repent all the moments of your life which you have wasted on pleasure. It is a sin of which, God knows, I, too, had been guilty; take courage and boldly reproach me with it.

I have indeed been your master, but it was only to teach you sin. You called me Father before I had any claim to the title, I deserved rather that of despoiler. I am your Brother, but it is the affinity of sin that brings me that distinction. I am called your husband, but only as the result of a public scandal. To do me honor and, in some way, to justify your own desires, you have ill treated the sanctity of so many terms in your letter. Erase them and

106

replace the praises you bestowed upon me with those of evildoer and traitor, who has conspired against your honor, destroyed your happiness and betrayed your innocence. This is the thought you ought to have of me!

I wish you could see me here with my drawn face, surrounded by menacing monks who are offended by my meager body, and who feel threatened by my castigating them for their evil ways.

I am determined this letter shall be my last fault. Should it be in God's design to deliver me into the hands of my enemies and should they prevail, have my body, wherever it may be found, above or below the earth, carried to the House of The Paraclete. You shall see me then, but not, as you fear, to cause you sorrow. The more grievous the afflictions of my life, the more you should desire to see me freed of them; you know for certain that whoever will deliver me from this life will deliver me from a heavy penalty. I do not know what lies in store for me thereafter, but there is no uncertainty as to that which I escape. You shall see me then, so that your devotion to Heaven may be strengthened by the sight of my lifeless body, and my death be eloquent to tell you what you brave when you love a man.

It would befit me to lie buried in your cemetery, for I know no place safer, more peaceful for a sorrowing soul. The constant sight of my sepulchre would also serve as a reminder of your duty: it will permit you and your daughters to pray to the Lord for my salvation at the close of every hour.

I beseech you, as much as my bodily well-being has heretofore concerned you, should that time come, show, above all else, your everlasting solicitude for the redemption of my soul!

Live and thrive! To you and your sisters I bid farewell!

TO HER MASTER ABELARD from his servant Heloise:

I read the letter I received from you, dearest Abelard, with great anxiety. I hoped to find nothing in it except words to soothe my grieving soul. I was, however, disturbed by the manner in which you addressed me in your letter: why did you place my name before yours? What does this unusual distinction mean? Why put the name of wife before that of the husband, or the servant before her master? The rule is to place the name of our superiors or our equals before our own, and when addressing others, the names appear in sequence of their prominence. It was your name only, the name of father and husband, which I eagerly sought. I did not look to find my own, which I would, if possible, forget, for it is the cause of your misfortune. The rules of decorum and your position as master and director over me require adherence to precedent in addressing me; besides, the nature of our relationship has become such, that formality is now indispensable; you know all this but too well! Let me ask you, did you address me thus before our separation had ruined my life?

I can see your heart has left me and you have made greater advances in the way of religious devotion than I could wish. Have you really abandoned me, Abelard? The uncertainty of this stabs my heart. The fearful prediction you make at the end of your letter, those terrible images you draw of your death, horrify me. How cruel of you! You ought to have quelled the turmoil of my heart and you throw it into greater confusion!

You desire that after your death I take care of your remains and pay them the last duties. Dear God! In what temper did you conceive these dreadful ideas and how could you so cryptically describe them to me? Did it not occur to you that you might cause my heart to stop and did that thought not make the pen drop from your hand? You did not reflect, I suppose, to what state of torment you were going to subject me? Heaven, severe as it has been to me, is not so insensible as to permit

110

me to live one moment after you. Life without you, Abelard, would be an insufferable punishment and death a joy, if, by that means, I could be united with you. If Heaven would listen to my cry, your days will be prolonged and you will bury me. Is it not within your realm to prepare me for that great crisis which shakes the most resolute and stable minds? Is it not your function to receive my last sighs, to preside at my funeral and give an account of my acts and my faith? Who but you can recommend me worthily to God and by the fervor and merit of your prayers conduct to Him my soul, which you had joined to His worship by solemn vows? I expect those pious offices from your paternal generosity. Thereafter you will be free from those disquietudes which now plague you and you will quit life with ease whenever it shall please God to call you. You may follow me then, content with what you have done for me and in full assurance of the well-being of my soul. But until that moment arrives, do not remind me of the inevitable, for I have had my share of unhappiness and see no need for having my sorrows increased. My life here is but a languishing death; would you hasten it? As it is,

111

my purgatorial endeavors occupy my thoughts continually; must I seek in the future new reasons for fear? "How void of reason are men," said Seneca, "to ruin the present by reflecting on future evils!"

When you have finished your course here on earth, you said it is your desire that your body be carried to the House of The Paraclete, where it would always be before my eyes and ever present in my mind. Can you think that the scars you have made on my heart can ever be removed, or that any length of time can obliterate the memories we hold here of you? And where shall I find time for those prayers you speak of? I shall be occupied with other cares and so heavy a burden would leave me no free moment! Could my feeble reason endure such powerful assaults? If I were thus disturbed, I might rage against God Himself; He would not be softened by my cries, rather, He would be provoked by my reproaches. How should I pray or how should I bear up under my grief? I should be more eager to follow you than to attend to the ceremonies of your funeral. It is for you, Abelard, that I have resolved to live and if you are taken from me, I could make no possible use of my days. What lamentations should I make if Heaven, by a cruel pity, preserved me for that moment? When I but think of this final separation I feel all the agonies of death itself; what should become of me if I should see that dreadful hour? Refrain, therefore, from bringing to mind such devastating images, if not for the sake of affection, at least for pity.

You commend me to devote myself to my duty, and to be wholly God's, to Whom I am consecrated. How can I, when you frighten me with apprehensions that continually occupy my thoughts? When an evil threatens us and it is impossible to ward it off, why do we surrender to the unprofitable fear of it, which invariably is more tormenting than the evil itself? What have I to look forward to, after I have lost you? What can I hope for? What can confine me to earth when death shall have taken from it all I cherish? I have renounced my life, but kept unbroken the bonds of my love and the secret pleasure of incessantly thinking of you, in the knowledge that you are alive. But—you do not live for me, and I dare not hope that I shall see you ever again. This is, of all my sorrows, the most bitter one to bear.

Fate, merciless Fate! Have you not persecuted me enough? Will you give me no respite? You have exhausted all your vengeance upon me alone and have none left whereby you may appear cruel to others! Why this constant struggle against me? The wounds you have inflicted cover me completely and leave no space for more, unless it is your wish to end my life, or do you yet preserve me from death in order to prolong my suffering? Was ever any being so miserable? I had been raised to a state of perfect joy, only to be thrown into the depths of utter despair. But then, my fate has always been in extremes; nothing could compare with my happiness and now nothing can equal my anguish.

That those tragic events began at a time when we were innocent, when we seemed the least to deserve them, aggravates my unhappiness even more. While we lived in sin and gave ourselves to the pleasures of an illicit love, nothing hindered our way of life; but scarcely had we taken refuge in the sanctity of matrimony, when the wrath of Heaven fell upon us.

114

We were joined in holy wedlock before the altar, dear Abelard—should this not have given us God's protection from our enemies? Moreover, we lived in separate quarters; you were busy with your lectures at school and I, as you know, had retired to a cloister. I spent entire days in meditating on holy lessons, to which, in obedience to you, I had promised to apply myself. At this juncture, punishment befell us and you, who were the least guilty, received the brunt of all vengeance. You paid with your body for the sins we both had committed.

How ruthless was the punishment my uncle's henchmen had inflicted upon you! And who, in the name of Heaven, had given him that right over us? But why should I rage at Fulbert? I, wretched I, to have been put on this earth to cause so great a crime!

How dangerous it is for great men to permit themselves to be moved by our sex! They ought from infancy to be immune to sensibilities of the heart against all our charms. "Hearken, my son," quoting a proverb, "if a beautiful woman by her glances tries to entice you, do not permit yourself to be swayed, reject the sugar-coated pill she offers. Do not take the path she would

115

have you follow. Her house is the gate of decline." After careful consideration I have concluded that a beautiful woman often means disaster. She is the shipwreck of liberty, an entanglement from which a man is often incapable of freeing himself.

It was a woman who caused the downfall of the first man in the Garden of Eden; she, who was created to partake of his happiness, was the cause of his ruin. And how bright would have been the glory of Samson, had he not succumbed to the charms of Delilah—a lone woman disarmed him, the conqueror of armies; he saw himself delivered into the hands of the Philistines and deprived of his eyes. He died distracted, despairing, without any consolation —save that he took his enemies with him to their death.

Solomon, of whose wisdom princes had come from all parts of the world to partake, forsook pleasing God so that he might please women. That king, who had been chosen to build the temple, abandoned the worship of the very shrines he had raised and proceeded to such a pitch of folly as to burn incense to idols. And there was Job, who had no enemy more cruel

116

than his wife—what temptations did he not bear? The evil spirit, who had declared himself his persecutor, employed a woman as the instrument of his betrayal.

That same evil spirit made me an instrument to destroy you, Abelard. Although I am greatly guilty, I am also completely innocent, for when I agreed to become your wife, it was not with the intent to do you harm. As you well know, I have not misled you, but it was my devotion which has caused your downfall. If I have committed a sin in loving you so immeasurably, I cannot repent it. I have aimed to please you even at the expense of my virtue; as soon as I was convinced of your feelings, I yielded to your solemn affirmations without a moment's hesitation. To be loved by you, Abelard, was gladness to the utmost. So impatiently did I desire it, that at first I could not believe it was real. I made no use of that defense of honor which tyrannizes our sex; I sacrificed all to the affection I bore for you and I considered it my duty, nay, it became my ambition, to please the foremost scholar of the age.

If any consideration had been able to stop me, it would without doubt have been my love

for you. I feared having nothing more to offer—
your feelings might then become languid and
you might seek new conquests. But it was easy
for you to cure me of that suspicion. I ought
to have foreseen other, more painful evils and
to have at least considered the possibility that
a love, gone amiss, could darken my whole
existence.

How glad should I be, could I wash away
with tears the memory of that time which still
delights me! At least I will try by strenuous
efforts to smother in my heart those desires to
which the frailty of my nature gives birth, and
I will subject myself to such torments as those
you have to suffer at the hands of your enemies.
I will strive by this means to atone at least to
you, even if I cannot appease an angry God.
My repentance is far from being complete, and
to show you the deplorable condition to which
I have been reduced, I dare to accuse God,
even at this moment, of cruelty, for leading
you into the snares your foes had prepared for
you. I am aware, my discontent can only kindle
divine wrath, when, as you admonished, I
should be asking for mercy.

In order to expiate a crime, it is not sufficient

to bear the punishment. Whatever we suffer is of no avail, if the passion still continues and the heart is filled with the same desire. It is an easy matter to confess a weakness and inflict on ourselves some punishment, but it requires perfect control over our nature to extinguish the memories of exhilarating delights, once they have gained possession of our minds. How many persons do we know who make an outward confession of their faults, yet, far from intending to correct them, take pleasure in relating them. Contrition of the heart ought to accompany the confession which crosses the lips, yet this very rarely happens.

I, who have experienced so many pleasures in loving you, feel, in spite of myself, that I cannot repent them, nor forgo the joy of reliving them in my memory. Whatever efforts I make, in whatever direction I turn, sweet thoughts still pursue me and every object brings to my mind what it is my duty to forget. During the quiet night, when my heart ought to be still in that sleep which suspends all our cares, I cannot avoid the illusions of my heart. I dream I am near you, I see you, I speak to you and hear your answers. Then we forsake all studies and give ourselves to each other. Sometimes too, I seem to struggle with your foes and then I break into piteous cries. The next moment I awaken in tears. Even into holy places, before the Lord's table, I carry the memory of our love and far from lamenting having been seduced, I sigh for having lost you, dear Abelard.

I remember well the time and place in which you first declared your love and swore you would cherish me till death. Your words, your oaths, are deeply graven in my heart and your name is for ever on my lips. Oh Lord, when I am thus afflicted, why dost not Thou pity my weakness and strengthen me?

You are fortunate, Abelard, in that your misfortune has enabled you to find rest. The punishment of your body has cured the tempest within your soul and driven you into a quiet haven. God, who seemed to deal heavily with you, in reality sought only to help you; he was a Father chastising and not an enemy revenging —he was a wise physician putting you through some pain in order to preserve your life.

I am much more to be pitied, for I still have a thousand emotions to conquer. That, which you have suffered in body for a passing hour,

120

I may suffer in anguish of soul throughout my life. I must resist those fires which passion kindles in a young body; I am weak and I have the greater difficulty in defending myself, because the very enemy who attacks me, pleases me—I am fond of the danger which threatens. How then can I avoid yielding?

In the midst of these struggles I try at least to conceal my weakness from those you have entrusted to my care. All who are about me admire my virtue; they believe virtue is purity of the flesh; but could their eyes penetrate into my heart, what would they not discover? My feelings there are in rebellion; I preside over others, but cannot rule myself. I have a false covering and my apparent virtue is but vice. Virtue should be an affair of the spirit as well as of the body. Men judge me praiseworthy, but I am guilty before God; before His all-seeing eye nothing is hidden and I cannot escape. It is a great effort for me, merely to maintain a semblance of virtue. Hypocrisy in this instance, is commendable. I give no scandal to the world which so eagerly seeks to cast aspersions; I do not shake the virtue of those feeble ones who are under my rule. With a heart full of love for a man, I teach them only to love God. With a soul overwhelmed by the gratification of love, I attempt to prove that these pleasures are all vanity and deceit. Fortunately, I have just adequate strength to conceal my longings, and I look upon that as a gift of divine grace. Although it is not enough to make me embrace virtue, it suffices to keep me from committing sin.

And yet it is futile to try and separate these two things: they must be guilty who do not practice righteousness—and they depart from virtue who delay defending it. Besides, we ought to have no other motive than the love of God. What then can I hope for? I add to my confusion a fear of offending a man rather than of provoking God, and I study less to please Him than to please you. Yes, it was only your command, and not a sincere vocation which sent me into these cloisters; I sought to give you ease and not to sanctify myself. I tear myself away from all that pleases me; I bury myself alive; I exercise myself with the most rigid fastings and all those severities which our laws impose upon us; I feed myself with tears and sorrows; but despite all of this, I can gain nothing by my expiation. My false piety has long deceived you as well as others; you have thought me at peace, when I was more disturbed than ever. You persuaded yourself I was wholly devoted to my duty, yet I had no other thought but love for you. Under this mistaken notion you desire my prayers—dear Abelard, I need yours! Do not presume upon my virtue. I may well have perished before your helping hand can reach me. We have to fear the present, especially, because I am weakening and can no longer find relief in you.

What reason had you to praise me? Praise can be very harmful to those on whom it is bestowed; hidden vanities appear, blind us and conceal from us the wounds that are half healed. A seducer flatters while betraying us, whereas a sincere friend disguises nothing, and far from passing a light hand over our wounds, makes us feel them the more intensely by applying remedies. Why do you not deal in this manner with me? Will you be a common and lowly flatterer? Or, if by chance, you see anything commendable in me, have you no fear that vanity, which comes so naturally to women, should quite efface it? But let us by no means

123

judge virtue by its outward appearances, for then the outcast, as well as the chosen, may lay claim to it. An impostor may, by his command of words and his skillful misrepresentation, gain more admiration than an honest man.

The heart of a woman is a labyrinth whose windings are very difficult to discover. The praises you give me are the more to be feared because I love the person who bestows them. The more I desire to please you, the more ready I am to believe the merit you attribute to me. Therefore, think instead how to unnerve me by wholesome reprimands and, rather than being confident, be fearful of my salvation. Say that they only will be crowned, who have fought with the greatest difficulties to the end. I seek not the crown—I am content if I can avoid danger. It is easier to stand aside than to win a battle. Yes, there are various degrees of happiness and I am not ambitious to attain the highest; I leave that to those of greater courage. I seek not to conquer, for fear I might fail. Happiness, for me, is to escape shipwreck and at last reach port. If God will reserve a little place in Heaven, He will have done enough for me. Up there, there is no envy, everyone is content with whatever he receives. Heaven commands me to renounce this fatal devotion to you. But no, my heart will never be able to consent to that! Farewell!

F O U R T H   L E T T E R

To her Master, Abelard, from Heloise:

Dear Abelard—Perhaps you expect me to accuse you of negligence. You have not answered my last letter and thanks to Heaven, the way I feel and the condition in which I find myself today, it is a relief to me that you display so much insensibility to the feelings I have shown you. At last, Abelard, I have banished you from my thoughts. The lover I once adored matters no more. His image will no longer pursue me. No longer shall I remember the man of mark and merit, the wonder of the age in whose fame I gloried! This news, without doubt, will surprise you. As you must always have known, I had been prejudiced by such a strong inclination toward you, it is hard to conceive that even the passage of time could alter this state.

But solitude becomes unbearable to an uneasy mind and the longer one endures it, the greater one's problems loom. Since I have been shut off from the outside world, I have done little but reminisce; especially of late. Calling the past to mind is not without pain to me. Yes, dear Abelard, only the silent walls of this cloister bear witness to my unhappiness. Like a wretch condemned to eternal slavery, I have worn out my days with bitterness. Instead of fulfilling God's merciful designs toward me, I have offended Him by looking upon this sacred refuge as a frightful prison. If I dare rely upon my feelings, I have again made myself worthy of your esteem. You are to me no longer the loving Abelard, who, in Fulbert's house, sought private conversations with me and deftly deceived the vigilant servants hovering about us. You are now Abelard, the true Penitent! Our experience gave you a horror of sin and you lost no time in consecrating the rest of your life to virtue and willingly submitting to it. I, indeed more eager and more attuned to the feelings of the heart, bore this kind of existence with extreme impatience. You have seen my resentment towards Providence and it was this, I dare say, which caused you to lose your regard for me. Doubtlessly you are alarmed at my grumblings against God in my last letter and, if the truth be told, despaired of my salvation. You could not predict that I would conquer such deep emotions; but you see, you were mistaken, Abelard—my feelings have not kept me from winning this battle. Restore me, then, to your good graces; your own piety should urge you to this.

Henceforth you have nothing to fear, for at last I can see the futility of that happiness upon which we had set our hearts. The scene has changed, solitude seems to me more acceptable and I am more receptive to the peace of this retreat, in which I now feel elated in the satisfaction of performing my duty. My peace has indeed cost me dear; I have bought it at the price of my innermost feelings and offered to God a sacrifice I thought beyond all my power. Perhaps I am unreasonably afraid; virtue directs all my acts and they are all subject to forgiveness. Therefore have no fear, Abelard, I no longer have those sentiments of which I wrote and which had given you so much distress. I will no longer try, by recalling the joyful moments of the past, to awaken whatever guilty fondness you may have felt for me. Forget the titles of Lover and Husband and keep only that

129

of Father. I expect no longer those tender declarations, so essential to feed the flame of love. I demand nothing of you but spiritual advice. The path of repentance, however thorny it be, will yet appear agreeable to me, if, under your guidance, I may walk in your footsteps. You will always find me ready to follow you. I shall also read with greater constancy the letters in which you describe the advantages of virtue, than I did those in which you so artfully aroused my passion. But if I have torn you from my heart, Abelard, be content with having a place in my mind which you shall never lose; I shall always take secret pleasure in thinking of you and shall consider myself fortunate in obeying the rules you will give me.

What held true yesterday, when I interrupted these lines, does not hold true today; new troubles rise in my soul. Unthought-of emotions appear to oppose the resolution I had formed, to tear you from my heart. God had overtaken me and I solemnly promised to be faithful to my vows—now I am perjured once more. This sacrilege fills the measure of my iniquity and God will not forgive, for I have tired out His forgiveness. Now I grieve for you again, when

130

I ought rather to regard our misfortune as a gift of Heaven, which had disapproved of our engagement and parted us.

Nevertheless, were you to remain voiceless once more, you would be gravely at fault. Formerly, when desire roused you, your letters were frequent and they came on eagles' wings, but now, when I so painfully long for you and press you so urgently to write to me, you wrap yourself in silence. In my misery you deny me the only comfort which is left me, that solace which only a word from you can bring. You think it injurious to my soul; you ignore my pleas and encourage severities to force me to forget you.

This very moment I received a letter from you; I will read it and answer it forthwith. I thank you for expressing concern for my health. Yours, you tell me, is failing and you thought lately you were going to die. With what indifference you tell me a thing so certain to hurt me! I told you how I would feel, should you leave this earth and, if you have any consideration for me, you will moderate the rigors of your austere life. But let me not tire you with repetitions!

131

You mentioned again that you desire us not to forget you in our prayers; no, dear Abelard, you may depend upon the zeal of this society, it is devoted to you and you cannot, in truth, fear its forgetfulness. You are our Father and we are your children; you guide us and we resign ourselves to your direction. You command and we obey; we faithfully execute what you have prudently ordered. Nothing is thought to be proper here, which has not received your approbation.

You tell me one thing that perplexes me— that you have heard some of our sisters are bad examples and they are generally not strict enough. Ought this to seem strange to you who know how monasteries are filled nowadays? Do fathers consult the inclination of their children when they settle them in religious communities? Are not parents primarily motivated by their own selfish interests, rather than the happiness of their daughters? It is for this reason monasteries are often filled with those who become a scandal to them. But may I ask what the irregularities are, of which you have heard and let me, at the same time, ask you to show me the proper remedy for them. I have not yet

132

observed any looseness here; when I do, I will take due care. I walk my rounds every night and make those I find outside return to their chambers, for I remember well the incidents which occurred in that monastery near Paris.

You end your letter with a general deploring of your unhappiness and the wish for death, to end a weary life. Is it possible so great a genius cannot rise above himself? What would people say, should they become aware of the letters you wrote? Would they consider the noble motive of your retirement, or rather think you had sought the solitude of a monastery for the purpose of bemoaning your fate? What would your young students say, if they should discover you are a mere victim of those weaknesses from which your teachings try to secure them? This man they so much admire would lose their admiration and become the sport of his pupils.

If these reasons do not suffice, look at me, with what determination I buried myself behind these cloister walls, only because you had demanded it. I was young when we separated and, if I can believe what you had often told me, worthy of any man's affections. Had I loved nothing but carnal pleasures, other men might have gratified me. God knows I had given you ample assurances of my undying love, I dried your tears with gentle kisses and, because you were unnerved and vulnerable, I became less reserved. Yes, if you had loved with purity of heart, you would have kept in mind the oaths I made, and remembered the tenderness with which I had surrounded you. All of this should have reassured you. Had you seen me grow indifferent after that infamous attempt on your life, you might have had reason to despair; but you never received greater tokens of my affection than during that period of our lives.

Let me see no more in your letters, dear Abelard, such murmurs against Fate. Heaven knows you are not the only one who has felt her blows and you ought to forget her outrages. What a shame it is that a philosopher cannot accept what might befall any man. Again, let me be an example—I was born full of vigor and passion, and yet I subjugate them both to reason. Must a lesser mind fortify one that is so much superior?

Is it thus I write to my dear Abelard? He who practices all the virtues he preaches? If you rail against Fate, it is not so much that you feel her blows, as that you try to show your enemies how much they are responsible for your misfortunes. Leave them, dear Abelard, leave them to exhaust their malice and continue to enthrall your audiences. Discover those treasures of learning Heaven seems to have reserved for you; your enemies, struck with the splendor of your reasoning, will, in the end, do you justice. Your learning is generally accepted, your greatest adversaries admit you are ignorant of nothing the mind of man is capable of knowing.

My dear Husband, for the last time I use that title! Shall I never see you again? Shall I never have the pleasure of embracing you before death? Alas, the love we once shared was so sweet that I can feel no regrets, nor do I wish to dismiss it from my memory. In truth, it is to you I owe the greatest happiness in my retirement: after having passed the day thinking of you, night falls and I go to sleep, full of forbidden thoughts. It is then that I give myself to you completely. What joy, dear Abelard! I see you in these moments and I hear your voice. How my eyes behold you tenderly! Some times you tell me of your plight and fill my soul with sadness; at other times our enemies are forgotten and you press me to your heart and I yield to your embrace. The very movements of my body betray the thoughts of my soul and I utter words which I ought not to speak. Even in the solemnity of early morning mass, when prayers should be purest, these immodest images pursue me. Delightful dreams and tender illusions! How soon you vanish! I awaken and open my eyes to find no Abelard; I stretch out my arms to embrace him and he is not there; I cry and he hears me not! Oh Lord, instead of deploring my transgressions, I grieve for what I have lost!

How unwise of me to reveal my dreams to you who are now insensible to such feelings! Do you ever see me in your sleep, Abelard? How do I appear to you? Do you entertain me in the same tender fashion as you did formerly and are you pleased or sorry when you awaken? But no, I must no longer expect from you the correspondence of desire. We have bound ourselves to severe austerities and must follow them at all costs. Let us think of our rules and our duties and make good use of that necessity which keeps us apart. You, Abelard, will happily finish your life; your desires and ambitions will be no obstacle to your salvation. But I must weep, without ever knowing whether my tears have been to any avail.

I cannot end this letter without telling you what occurred here a few days ago. A young nun who had been forced to enter the convent, although she had no inclination for sacrificing herself to God, escaped to England with a man. I have ordered everyone in the house to conceal the matter. Abelard, if you were near us, such incidents would not happen, for the sisters would be inspired by your presence, faithfully practice their rules and follow your directions. The young woman would never have contemplated so unfortunate a design as that of breaking her vows, had you been here to guide us. Yes, had your eyes been witness to our actions, they would all be acceptable to God and, sure of foot, we would walk in the path of the virtuous.

I begin to perceive, Abelard, that I take too much pleasure in writing to you; I ought to burn this letter. It shows how deeply I feel for you yet, and that my affection has not diminished, though at the beginning of this letter I tried to persuade you otherwise. As you can see, I am subject to waves of both purity and passion, and by turns I yield to each. I implore you, do not withdraw again and in some measure make my last days as peaceful, as my first have been disturbed and turbulent!

To HELOISE from Abelard:

Write to me no more, Heloise, write no more! It is time we end those communications which render our penances meaningless. We retired from the world to purify ourselves. Let us not forget that by our conduct, directly contrary to religious morality, we had become odious to the Lord! Let us no longer deceive ourselves about our past; it but serves to spoil our solitude.

You say we are innocent and you blame God for our unjust punishment. I most vehemently disagree with this old and quarrelsome complaint of yours! What happened to us was well deserved, even though we were wedded at the time chastisement befell us. I will grant you our marriage bond rendered our relation no longer illicit; but were we not guilty of the most disgraceful misconduct preceding our marriage? Would this alone not have called for the severest punishment? And after we were married and you had gone to Argenteuil to keep our union a secret, mut I remind you how furtively I used to visit you there? I am sure you recall those nights in that sanctified corner in the refectory, where I sacrificed our bodies and shamefully vented my unbridled passion on you. And when you took exception and tried to resist and attempted to turn me from my purpose, did I not frequently overpower you, thus forcing your consent? Neither respect for decency nor respect for God restrained me from wallowing in the mire, even at times set aside for solemn prayers. I was tied to you by such ardor and burned with such desire that even today the mere thought of those despicable pleasures makes me blush.

People indeed were not wrong in saying that when we separated, it was shame and grief that made me abandon the world; it was not, as you know, a sincere repentance for having offended God. Now I consider our misfortune a secret design of Providence to punish our sins, and I look upon Fulbert merely as an instrument of divine vindication. Remember that I had betrayed him in a most contemptible manner long before he took his revenge on me.

140

Having endured the rage of my foes and all their persecutions, I have no doubt that God Himself raised them in order to purify me. In His divine wisdom, He has chastised us only to save us from the abyss.

I should be happy indeed, if I had none to fear but my enemies, and no other hindrance to the salvation of my soul but their slander. But, Heloise, you make me tremble, your letters declare that you are enslaved by human desire —reflect then, if you cannot conquer it, you cannot be saved. What part would you have me play in your trial before the Supreme Judge?

No, let us be more firm in our resolutions! Attempt to break these shameful chains which bind you to the senses! Try, with all your strength, to be a model of perfection. It is difficult, I will admit, but it is not impossible. If your first efforts prove weak, do not give way to despair, for that would be cowardice. To subdue the affection of the heart you first have to overcome the desires of the flesh; be not surprised, then, by the power of your inclinations! Stand fast and beware, you are dealing with a cunning adversary who will use all means

141

to seduce you. Temptation, it is written, is forever with us.

Be strong, Heloise, and when desire arises, stifle it at its inception, let it not take root in your heart! Temptations have their degrees, they are at first mere thoughts and appear harmless; the imagination receives them without any fears; the pleasure grows, we dwell upon it and finally we yield.

Heloise, you are at the head of a society and you know there is a difference between those who lead a private life and those who are charged with the conduct of others. The first need only labor for their own well-being and in their round of duties are not obliged to practice all the virtues publicly; but those who have the charge of others entrusted to them ought, by their example, to encourage their followers to do all the good of which they are capable.

Yes, Heloise, avoid, by a pure life, the punishment prepared for sinners. I dare not give you a description of those dreadful torments which are the consequences of a life of guilt. I am filled with horror when they present themselves to my imagination. Heloise, I can conceive of nothing which can describe the tor-

142

tures of the damned; the fire we see upon this earth is but the shadow of that which burns them.

Hereafter, apply yourself to the earnest pursuit of your salvation, it ought to be your sole concern. Banish me, therefore, forever from your mind—it is the best advice I can give you.

Farewell, these are my last instructions. Heaven grant that your heart, once so abandoned to my wants, will now yield to my council. May your image of the loving Abelard be now that of Abelard truly penitent; and may you shed as many tears for your soul as you have shed over the loss of our sinful past.

Adieu!

CONCLUSION

As FAR AS IS KNOWN, only two additional letters, both regarding purely monastic matters, passed between them. Time and physical mutilation had taken their heavy toll. Abelard, consumed by the desire to purify his soul, wanted neither to respond to Heloise's emotional demands nor to be reminded of the past. There was no vestige of feeling left for the woman he once pursued and he remembered with dismay the love he had felt for her in earlier days.

As for Heloise, who realized the futility of her attempts to rekindle old feelings, she no longer wrote of personal concerns. Instead, she now asked for instruction in the conduct of nuns and for enlightenment on the origin of religious communities for women. It was a request the founder and spiritual director of her institution could hardly refuse. It was also her final try at keeping her contact with her husband alive. He answered in great detail, but the strict guidelines he wrote for her unmis-

takably point to a maneuver to keep her isolated and, even at this late date, to keep her
contact with the outside world curtailed. Their
correspondence ended therewith, but Abelard's
troubles continued.

In 1135, after seven agonizing years of strife,
he fled from the monks of St. Gildas. One year
thereafter, during which he probably toiled on
his later published works, we find him back on
the familiar slope of Stê. Genevieve with his
students.

We do not know by whose authority he resumed his lectures, but it is worthy of note that
among his pupils were, as in the past, future
cardinals, bishops and legates. In short, Abelard
again attracted the outstanding minds of his
day in extraordinary numbers.

Had the scholar chosen to remain in the
hinterlands of Brittany, or had he continued
to live his life in a less visible manner, his
enemies would probably have gone no further.
But when, back in Paris, the effectiveness of
his teaching began to tell and the schools of
his rivals began to empty once more, his antagonists went into action. Leading the pack
of his pursuers was Bernard of Clairvaux. The

self-proclaimed defender of faith, an ascetic and zealous monk, had long eyed Abelard's rationalism with intense suspicion. "He watched the Church of God with fierce zeal! . . . he knew everything and everybody; smote archbishops and kings as freely as his own monks; hunted down every heretic that appeared in France in his day; played even a large part in the politics of Rome."[44] This is an apt description of the saintly Bernard, who pretended to have been an innocent bystander in the affair rather than the relentless persecutor of Abelard that he really was. He wanted the world to believe it was chance which had drawn him into the dispute with the renowned master; that he had become involved only after William of St. Thierry, a friend and former abbot of Rheims, had urgently requested he look into the theologically damaging statements of the scholar's and had insisted he take appropriate action. Nothing could be further from the truth! The confrontation between these two antagonists was long years in the making. In fact, there are historians who insist that even the letter from William of St. Thierry was a sham, that it had actually been written by Bernard himself.

147

While there were no outright heresies in Abelard's work, parts in his writings could lend themselves to such a charge. The scholar's assertion that all dogma be subject to logical explanation, and that the mystery in religion should be able to withstand rational scrutiny, was intended by Abelard to strengthen the position of the Church by answering hitherto unanswerable questions. Bernard, on the other hand, perceived the questioning of belief not only as blasphemy, but as a denial of faith, and as a corruptive influence on the young and on the simple-minded.

We are now in the year 1140—the great ecclesiastical Council of Sens was about to convene. Convinced that his writings were well within the bounds of orthodoxy, Abelard wrote to the archbishop of Sens demanding to be heard before the upcoming assembly, and to be permitted to defend himself against the charges of heresy propagated about him.

It was not long before the archbishop was to respond in the affirmative; he also invited Bernard to participate in the theological disputation. Debating the foremost dialectician of his day, however, was not what Bernard had

148

in mind. He declined the challenge, explaining he was totally unprepared and would be "a mere child"[45] in the art of dialectics, pitted against so persuasive and articulate an opponent as Abelard. Nonetheless, the bishops and prelates whom Bernard had mobilized to defend the faith prevailed upon him to attend the Council. Whether or not Bernard's initial refusal to go to Sens was mere posturing remains a moot point. Rémusat believed that even if Bernard was not ready to confront Abelard in debate, he had certainly prepared for the verdict. The list of "heresies" Bernard would produce at the forthcoming council not only consisted of passages taken out of context from Abelard's writings, but he had added some which had not even come from the scholar's pen.

And that was not all. Bernard's exhortations, the day before the great meeting had begun, left the citizens of Sens so irate and aroused against Abelard that, when on the street, he had to keep out of sight for fear of being stoned. The situation was strikingly similar to what had occurred nineteen years earlier at Soissons. However, at Soissons Abelard had friends

149

among the judges; at Sens, those who had once favored him were now apprehensive of Bernard's power and deserted the scholar. Possibly Geoffrey, Bishop of Chartres, was one who could have been counted on to be impartial, but even he appeared to have faltered under the forceful influence of the Abbot of Clairvaux. To put things in perspective we must remember that at the time Bernard was probably the most feared—and because of it, the dominant personage of the Church in France.

And so the day of the trial, June 4, 1140, dawned. "The Cathedral at Sens was filled with one of the strongest throngs that ever gathered within its venerable walls. Church and State and the schools had brought their highest representatives and their motley thousands to witness a thrilling conflict of the two first thinkers and orators of the land."[46] Except for the handful of companions Abelard had brought with him, he saw no friends among the surging crowd. Following the chanting of the clerics and the customary sermons, Bernard mounted the pulpit and began the proceedings. After reading the statements with which he accused Abelard, Bernard solemnly petitioned the Council to render a guilty verdict. To the amazement of the assembly Abelard thereupon rose and left the cathedral, declaring that he would acknowledge none but the Pope's determination and would journey to Rome to appeal. The interruption created great confusion, especially among the delegates, for whom the legality of it all was now brought into question: was it lawful to proceed with the trial in face of Abelard's appeal and in the absence of his person? Bernard fully assured the members of the Council that it was; whereupon they moved to condemn the disputed doctrines as heretical and dispatched a report to the Eternal City, informing Pope Innocent II of their action.

To shed some light on Abelard's extraordinary behavior, we have to look at the immediate circumstances. That Abelard feared the "rising of the people," at least that is what the Bishop of Freising suggested, was most likely not the case. That he was ill, possibly, yes—but not so ill as to lack the ability to defend himself. Finally, that he had lost his nerve when Bernard read the charges against him is conceivable, but not at all probable. The most likely explanation is that Abelard had learned of a secret meeting

151

Bernard had had with the bishops, during which they had decided, in advance, to render a guilty verdict. In summary, the scholar was well aware that his chances for a fair hearing were non-existent.

Bernard was now concerned that Abelard, who was known to have supporters in the Roman Curia, might well succeed in having the condemnation set aside. He therefore lost no time and left nothing to providence in using every possible means to have the verdict confirmed before the scholar could reach Rome.

While his fate was being sealed for him, Abelard still lingered in Paris. Bernard had launched so swift and massive a campaign, so insidious and vilifying, that whatever support the scholar might have hoped for was totally undermined. Pope Innocent was fully convinced of the validity of Bernard's claims and did not waver. On the 16th of July 1140, on the steps of St. Peter's, the decree of Abelard's excommunication was read: "that he remain perpetually silent, his works condemned to the flames and his person to be imprisoned by the ecclesiastical authorities."[47] Abelard had been condemned unheard.

The summer was almost over when, nearly destitute and unaware of his condemnation, Abelard set out in the direction of Rome. Covering the great distance on foot was a punishing effort for one bruised by so much conflict and dissent. There is no record of his progress along the way, save that one day he reached the Benedictine monastery of Cluny, near Mâcon, for his night's shelter. The abbot at the time was Peter the Venerable, a cultured man of patrician birth, possessed of "a fine and equable temper, high principle, gentle and humane feeling and much practical wisdom."[48] He was a powerful lord with far-reaching influence, controlling vast amounts of wealth. Peter commiserated with the scholar, received him in a spirit of compassion and offered the older man asylum in his abbey. The venerable Peter was, like Abelard, no friend of Bernard's, for he himself had felt his sting during an encounter a few years earlier and had not forgotten the outrageous assault the Abbot of Clairvaux had mounted against him. But Peter was not intimidated and had forcefully countered "the new race of Pharisees,"[49] as he called Bernard and his followers in a letter to the Pope.

It was at Cluny that Abelard first learned that the verdict of Sens had been confirmed. Still, he hoped to receive justice from the Roman Pontiff, and wished to continue on his journey. The venerable Peter, no newcomer to Church politics, well understood the scholar's dilemma and made every attempt to guide him to safer ground; primarily, to spare him the public humiliation which Bernard had demanded. He urged Abelard to abandon his pilgrimage, arguing that the Pope would never cast his vote against Bernard, even if the Breton were able to reach Rome and plead his case. With no other options left, the weary scholar would ultimately concede and accept Peter's generous offer to stay at Cluny.

Now history took a turn and the Abbot of Cluny became more urgently involved. First and foremost, Peter realized that in order to achieve some kind of an accommodation with the Pontiff, a means had to be found to diffuse Bernard's violent antagonism toward Abelard. With that in mind, Peter convinced the scholar to correct in his writings "all which is offensive to pious ears."[50] For one so proud as Abelard, such a compromise must have been an enormous effort. Though he had to yield some ground, he was not in a particularly remorseful mood, as the introductory note of his apology to Bernard would indicate: ". . . in those things for which I am so gravely charged, I am conscious of no fault, nor should I obstinately defend them if I were. It may be that I have erred in my writings, but I call God to witness and to judge in my soul that I have written nothing through wickedness or pride in those things for which I am chiefly blamed."[51] What Abelard had here committed to paper was an apology, not the recantation Bernard had sought; but the document had "a sufficient air of retraction about it to allow Bernard to withdraw."[52] It would also serve, with a few additional promises on Abelard's part, as the basis for their reconciliation. A few days later, in response to Peter's suggestion, Abbot Reynard of Cîteaux invited the two antagonists to come together at his monastery. The meeting took place and a reconciliation was effected. Abelard's sole reference to this crucial event was that it had been a "peaceful encounter."[53]

Abbot Peter now undertook the task of securing authorization for Abelard to remain at his abbey. The briefs he dispatched to Rome were masterpieces of diplomacy whose message Pope Innocent could not ignore. The answer was swift and positive: Abelard was granted permission to stay at Cluny and was allowed to join the ranks of the friars.

There was one more concession the prudent abbot would wring from the Pope: that the scholar shall not be harassed by any demand, and that he "might not be driven away or troubled by the importunity of any person."[54] Thus the sword of Damocles, which hung heavily above Abelard's head, had been removed. He was free now to spend what days were left him in quiet contemplation, in study, or to participate in the daily rituals of the abbey. But shattered in body and broken in spirit, devoid of all worldly aspirations, he had nothing more to say and there was little more for him to do, other than to prepare for that life which was to come.

Abelard had finally found what had evaded him throughout his life: at Cluny all was peace. But he was not to enjoy its benefits for long— as the months passed, his infirmities began to take a turn for the worse. Abbot Peter, ever solicitous of the scholar's needs, had him moved to the Priory of St. Marcel, a daughter-house of Cluny. The priory lay on the banks of the Saône near the city of Châlons, in Burgundy. It was a smaller complex and, with its milder climate, a more suitable place for a sick man.

Simple in his wants and vestments, condemning superficialities and all things unnecessary for the maintenance of life, Abelard remained busy with "things of the mind."[55] He took part in some of the abbey's rituals and, despite his ailments, was active until the end. Abelard died on the 21st of April, 1142, at the age of sixty-three, and was first interred at St. Marcel.

When Abbot Peter sent word of the scholar's death to Heloise and informed her of the monastery where he was buried, she replied by reminding the abbot of Abelard's wish that his body, "wherever it may be found, be carried to The Paraclete."[56]

The task with which she had confronted the abbot was not an easy one; the monks at St. Marcel, who had come to love the renowned scholar, were intent on keeping his remains and violently opposed the removal of the body from its resting place. But Abbot Peter had been a

157

great admirer of Heloise and could not find it
in his heart to deny her plea. Recalling the past,
he wrote "my affection for you does not begin
today, but dates from a long way back. I was
scarcely more than a boy, hardly a young man,
when the renown of your noble and praiseworthy studies reached me."[57] He went on to
say that he remembered her when she had
excelled among women and, young as she was,
her erudition had surpassed that of most men.
The venerable Peter had Abelard's body ex-
humed in secret and he himself accompanied it
to The Paraclete for burial.

Later, writing to Peter in a most gracious
manner and thanking him for all he had done,
Heloise mentioned her son Astrolabe for the
first and only time. She asked the abbot to
secure a prebend (a cathedral-related office)
for him. Peter acknowledged her request, but
there is no record to tell us whether his efforts
had met with success.

With Abelard's grave so near and all possible hope buried within it, Heloise assumed her
role as a religious with less distraction. But she
refused to become an ascetic; the prioress of

The Paraclete remained a woman in religious garb, for ever vowed to a man.

With all of Abelard's dire forecasts of horrors to come unless she ceased to profane her religion, Heloise had stood her ground. She never accepted his contention that God's judgment had been just, that the mutilation of his body was an act of divine charity. Likewise, Abelard had not been able to move her from her position that it was for him she bore the greater love, not for God, whom she outrightly accused of cruelty towards both of them. She also refused to retract her assertion that her penance at The Paraclete was for Abelard, not for God, whom she had not offended and to whom, therefore, she saw no need to atone.

In the twenty years that followed, The Paraclete became one of the most highly respected religious institutions in France. The convent's rules, originally laid down from directions formulated by St. Benedict, were the same as those for men. Heloise demanded concessions because the stringent regulations had neglected to take the more limited physical capacity of women into account; furthermore, the differing bodily functions of the female sex had been totally ignored. The statute concerning dress, for instance, stipulated a single set of clothing: an undergarment, a lamb skin, a woolen robe, and for the cold seasons a cape was allowed, which, if need be, could serve as a cover for the bed. Besides using these garments as daytime attire, the sisters had to sleep in their habits. Heloise had found the practice unacceptable and insisted they be allowed a second set of clothing, to enable the women to wash their habits and "keep vermin at bay."[58] Then there were the rules concerning feasting and abstinence and those regarding consumption of meat and the intake of wine. Even though Heloise saw these dietary laws as mere fringes rather than the essence of religious morality, she wanted them to be considered and put in their proper perspective. Directions for admitting clerics into the cloister for nightly prayer services needed to be clarified, as well as the rules for visiting churchmen and other dignitaries. It was one thing for an abbot to wine and dine guests at his table, but quite another, as Abelard knew only too well, for an abbess to entertain visitors in her abbey.

Heloise wanted reasonable and compassion-

160

ate guidelines from Abelard, to avoid the setting of excessive and unattainable goals. Above all she sought to minimize the inner conflicts certain to arise in those among her flock who were unable to live up to their commitments. Her particular concern was for girls who had been persuaded into religion and for those who, like herself, had entered a cloister without the knowledge of what such a life really entailed. With a few exceptions Abelard modified the rules and closely followed Heloise's proposals. These directions, with some additional modifications apparently added by Heloise in later years, remained in effect until the end of the eighteenth century, when the cloister was disbanded.

When Heloise died in the spring of 1163, she took her place beside her husband. Through all the storms and upheavals of the next eight centuries they have never been separated. What Heloise had most wanted to achieve in life, and what she had so desperately longed for, was not to be; but, as the irony of fate would have it, was granted her in death.

Though their grave was disturbed during the revolution and their remains moved several times, to this day they lie side by side in the cemetery of Père Lachaise in Paris, the burial ground of France's most famous children. No grave has been more revered, to echo Mark Twain, or more widely known and wept over in the Western World than this last resting place of Heloise and the man she loved. Even today, almost nine hundred years after their deaths, those holding fast to the memory of the tragic pair will place flowers upon their tomb, and often two people in love, or a grieving soul, will stand in front of the monument in silent homage. The poignant inscription, taken from their gravesite at The Paraclete, tells the final chapter of their journey.

"Here, beneath the same stone, repose of this monastery the founder, Peter Abelard, and the first Abbess, Heloise, heretofore in study, genius, love, ill-omened marriage, now in eternal happiness united."

ABELARD	HELOISE
April 21, 1142	May 17, 1163

N O T E S

1 Moncrieff.
2 Historia Calamitatum.
3 Ibid.
4 McCabe.
5 Ibid.
6 Ibid.
7 Historia Calamitatum.
8 Ibid.
9 Ibid.
10 McCabe.
11 Historia Calamitatum.
12 Ibid.
13 Ibid.
14 Ibid.
15 Ibid.
16 Ibid.
17 Ibid.
18 Morten.
19 Historia Calamitatum.
20 Ibid.
21 Astrolabe: A surveying instrument first used
by the Moors to solve problems in astronomy.
22 Historia Calamitatum.
23 Ibid.
24 Moncrieff.
25 Historia Calamitatum.
26 Ibid.
27 Ibid.
28 Ibid.
29 Ibid.
30 Ibid.

31 "Oh noble spouse,
What dire doom I moved when I thee wed,
And caused ill fortune to bow thy lofty head!
In sorrow now, here is the end—
I share thy fate with thee, in deep repent."
32 McCabe.
33 This and the preceding passage in quotes are
taken from the Historia Calamitatum.
34 Ibid.
35 McCabe.
36 Ibid.
37 Ibid.
38 Historia Calamitatum.
39 Ibid.
40 McCabe.
41 Historia Calamitatum.
42 McCabe.
43 This and the preceding passage in quotes are
taken from the Historia Calamitatum.
44 McCabe.
45 Ibid.
46 Ibid.
47 Ibid.
48 Ibid.
49 Ibid.
50 Ibid.
51 Ibid.
52 Ibid.
53 Ibid.
54 Ibid.
55 Gilson.
56 Abelard to Heloise, Second Letter.
57 Gilson.
58 Morten.

BIBLIOGRAPHY

THE LOVE LETTERS OF ABELARD AND HELOISE—Watts London—1722 (Reprinted 1901).

PETRI ABAELARDI—Opera, 2 vols. Victor Cousin, Paris—1849.

ABELARD, SA VIE, SA PHILOSOPHIE ET SA THEOLOGIE Charles de Rémusat, Paris—1855.

ABELARD AND THE ORIGIN AND EARLY HISTORY OF UNIVERSITIES—Gabriel Compayré—Charles Scribners Sons, New York—1893.

UNIVERSITIES OF EUROPE IN THE MIDDLE AGES H. Rashdall—Oxford Univ. Press—1895.

PETER ABELARD—Joseph McCabe—G.B. Putnam's Sons New York and London—1901.

THE LOVE LETTERS OF ABELARD AND HELOISE—The Temple Classics H. Morten (ed.) J. M. Dent, London—1901.

THE LOVE LETTERS OF ABELARD AND HELOISE—Ralph Seymour Fletcher, Chicago—1903.

BRIEFE VON ABELARD UND HELOISE—W. Fred—Insel Verlag Leipzig—1911.

HELOISE AND ABELARD—George Moore—Heinemann, London—1924.

THE LETTERS OF ABELARD AND HELOISE—C.K. Scott Moncrieff (transl.) Guy Chapman, London—1925.

PETER ABAILARD—J. G. Sikes—Cambridge University Press—1932.

THE STRICKEN LUTE—Roger B. Lloyd—Louat Dickson, Ltd. London—1932.

HELOISE DANS L'HISTOIRE ET DANS LA LEGENDE Charlotte Charrier, H. Champion, Paris—1933.

THE STORY OF CIVILIZATION, PART *IV*—Will Durant The Age of Faith, Simon and Schuster, New York 1950.

HELOISE AND ABELARD—Etienne Gilson—Henry Regnery Co. Chicago—1951.

FEUDAL SOCIETY—Marc Bloch—University of Chicago Press—1961.

THE STORY OF ABELARD'S ADVERSITIES—J. T. Muckle Pontif. Instit. of Med. Studies, Toronto—1964.